LEAN SUPPLY CHAIN MANAGEMENT

A HANDBOOK FOR STRATEGIC PROCUREMENT

by Jeffrey P. Wincel

Productivity Press
NEW YORK

Most Productivity Press books are available at quantity discounts when purchased in bulk. For more information contact our Customer Service Department (888-319-5852). Address all other inquiries to:

Productivity Press
444 Park Avenue South, 7th floor
New York, NY 10016
United States of America
Telephone: 212-686-5900
Telefax: 212-686-5411
E-mail: info@productivitypress.com
ProductivityPress.com

Composed by William H. Brunson Typography Services

Printed and bound by Malloy Lithographing in the United States of America

Library of Congress Cataloging-in-Publication Data

Wincel, Jeffrey.
Lean supply chain management : a handbook for strategic procurement / by Jeffrey Wincel.
p. cm.
ISBN 1-56327-289-X (alk. paper)
1. Business logistics. 2. Industrial procurement—Management. I. Title.
HD38.5.W56 2003
658.7'2—dc22

2003021131

09 08 07 06 5 4 3 2

There is only one person I can dedicate this to — Heather. Not only are you my partner in life, but my partner in spirit too. Without you, not only would this book have never happened, but neither would the joy of living life. Thank you and I love you.

Contents

Foreword

LEAN AND SUPPLY CHAIN IMPROVEMENTS

During the past 20 years, many manufacturing organizations in the U.S. have been writing and studying all aspects of lean manufacturing. The majority of these studies have been based on the famous Toyota Production System (TPS). These lean efforts have taken us in numerous directions. In many books, you can read about TPS, its various tools such as kanban and so on, and improvement techniques such as kaizen. Very little, however, has been written concerning one of the primary success reasons for this great system—supply chain management and development.

We have heard about the *kiritsu* of the Japanese OEMs, and assume this is another reason for success in Japan. Many believe that the joint ownership (and control) of suppliers by big corporations in a kiritsu allow companies such as Toyota to keep material prices and profits of suppliers down. This is one of our largest misunderstandings while studying lean manufacturing. Much more relevant is the constant joint analysis of the total value chain, and the rigorous effort to take waste out of the total system. These efforts are accomplished while *sharing* in the financial rewards made possible by the improvements in quality and profitability. Few have endeavored to put forward the value of utilizing the entire system approach complete with the tools of TPS and supply chain management in an understandable, applicable way.

Beyond reading about the supply chain approach from a successful company, the best learning advantage would be to supply companies like Toyota *and* traditional (automotive) companies. This would give an individual leader and teams the advantage of seeing and comparing the two methods, traditional versus lean, side by side. This side-by-side comparison enables us to see what works and what does not work in the U.S. manufacturing environment. This is exactly the comparison that Jeff Wincel brings to the table in his book, *Lean Supply Chain Management.*

Working for the "big three" automotive purchasing and supply chain organizations and major tier-one suppliers, Jeff had learned first hand the differences of these companies in their approach to supply chain management. Jeff used this as he set out to successfully incorporate the best practices into his team and their supply chain management efforts. In this book, Jeff examines the need to critically analyze the current business environment within a company and to recognize if a traditional (slow) change is acceptable, or if the company is in a crisis situation calling for rapid change. Each of these conditions will require different skills and application of lean implementation and supply chain management.

There is a degree of frustration in many organizations working to achieve the success of great companies like Toyota or Honda. This success includes improved quality, delivery, cost reduction, and team member morale, all aimed at the quest of improved profitability. There are continued efforts to study, read books, and employ consultants, but many companies are not seeing the expected bottom line of these efforts. One of the major problems with these efforts is the fact that leaders do not understand lean manufacturing as a total, fully integrated system of manufacturing the product, including the total material value chain. They tend to treat each tool of lean as an independent improvement potential. A second problem is that, all too often, the lean manufacturing system is thought of as a manufacturing-floor project using items like JIT, kaizen, and andons, but having little or no relationship to the total value chain. Likewise, in other corners of the company, total supply chain improvements are being studied independently from the greater total manufacturing systems being implemented. Jeff is one of the first to tie the critical relationships of a total lean manufacturing system (including the plant floor level tools) with the work on total value chain and supply base improvements.

Again, much has been written about the total value chain and true gains to be made in a cradle to grave value analysis by taking the waste out of the total system. This is nothing new. In the early 1900s, Henry Ford had a vision of accomplishing his mass production process with a vision of three days from raw material to finished product. Mr. Ford did this by understanding the total value chain from lumber, elements, and raw material through the entire supply base and into final assembly. He realized he could not achieve total cost reduction without a full concentration on the complete value stream. By the way, this was not known as a value steam in the 1900s—it was only sensible way to achieve total waste reduction and profit improvements while reducing the price of the product to the customer. Likewise, if you look very deeply at the Toyota Production System, or any successful lean system, you will need to realize that the company system goes far beyond the manufacturing floor and extends to the total value stream of suppliers. The system must incorporate the tools of lean manufacturing, aimed at improving the strength of the entire group by the reduction of waste. Jeff has worked to incorporate many of these tools.

Jeff, as the leader of purchasing and supply chain management for Donnelly Corporation, was very instrumental at working with the Donnelly Production System, also patterned after the Toyota system, and was highly successful at integrating the tools and techniques into the Donnelly distribution center and into the total supply chain. He used the annual planning system of lean to set targets for price reduction and other business improvement, but then extended the effort to assist and educate suppliers in the methods of working together for both companies' success. He was instrumental at ensuring that price reduction expectations were not a one-way street. The only way for us to have been successful was for both companies to succeed.

Many major manufacturers in many fields have not begun to grasp the need to work cooperatively with their suppliers to achieve real improvement. Their approach to price improvement, inventory control, or any other improvement is for the supplier to absorb all the cost, with the benefit only going to them as the customer. Even today, they are not seeing that this approach will not only destroy the supplier but also will not lead to cost reduction even in their own company. Jeff wants to take you in a completely different direction in his approach to understanding and approaching profit improvement through the total value chain.

Russ Scaffede
Vice President, Manufacturing
Tiara Yachts
Holland, Michigan

Introduction

WHY THIS BOOK AND WHY NOW?

With any new work, the question that always has to be answered is—*why? Why* a new book on supply chain management and procurement? *Why* another book about lean systems? *Why* should we care? Is there anything more important that we can learn from the concept of lean supply chain management?

Why a new book on supply chain management? The answer is simply because the works that exist tend to treat SCM as product movement and delivery, and SCM is really something greater than that. In fact, many books state that SCM is the same as logistics management,[1] using the Council of Logistics Management definition. Practitioners in SCM will undoubtedly tell you there are very unique differences between logistics and supply chain management. Throughout this book we revisit this difference and demonstrate how integrating SCM into other business elements delivers the greatest improvements of performance—with, yes, financial benefits as well!

Why a new book on lean? Most books on lean systems center on manufacturing operations and material management within that environment. These books describe the tools and methods by

1. David Simichi-Levi, Philip Kaminsky, and Edith Simichi-Levi, *Designing & Managing the Supply Chain: Concepts, Strategies, and Cases,* 2nd ed. p. xx. (New York: McGraw-Hill/Irwin, 1999)

which to implement lean initiatives, the measures by which success is observed, and the support needed to allow for implementation success. What they don't address is the pre-implementation events that need to occur in the supply chain to enable the lean efforts within the four walls. This is where the value of practical experience comes to play in how this question is answered. Linking supply chain efforts with lean efforts—really making them one and the same—is the way in which both efforts are optimized. So while this book addresses the use of lean tools and the integration with lean implementation internally, it really creates a new definition and practice in lean.

Why should we care? Again, the answer is simple, cost . . . or, more important, profit. In a typical manufacturing firm, procurement and supply chain costs make up about 50 percent of COGS (cost of goods sold), and manufacturing contributes 30 percent. Improvement in these two factors can provide the single biggest opportunity for profit improvement. At a 20 percent gross profit, it takes $5 of improved sales to equal the profit effect of $1 of supply chain savings. While most readers of this work will be either SCM practitioners or students, the truth of this story needs to be heard by the executive management of our organizations so that the appropriate focus and effort is placed here. Typically, organizations rally around sales strategies or overhead reduction strategies for improving profit, with this biggest piece of SCM being lost.

Finally, does this or any book provide the roadmap to integrate SCM strategy into the larger business strategy of a company? Many SCM initiatives have either been only moderately successful, or have completely failed. Why? They've failed because they haven't been part of a corporate strategy other than saving money. The tendency is that these plans are stand-alone, not usually an extension of the company's manufacturing or technology plans, and may in fact be in direct conflict with the company's goals and approach. This book was written specifically to be used as a strategic planning tool in developing a world class supply chain and procurement plan.

This book doesn't jump immediately to implementation steps, but builds the overall business and value systems that must be in place first. It addresses the different commercial and financial environments in which an organization might find itself, and recommends specific approaches tailored to those conditions. Finally, the book concludes by focusing on the SCM steps and implementation order that facilitates the implementation of lean manufacturing within your own organization.

WHAT'S IN THIS BOOK?

A number of major themes are covered throughout this book, building on many of the current trends in SCM and integrating them into the plan and practice of world class SCM. Among these issues is the use of e-business tools to facilitate efficiency and improvement in the tactical transactions, and strategic planning elements in delivering the plan to implementation. The promise of these e-business solutions often outpaces the reality of their effectiveness and availability. However, when the fundamentals of sound procurement and SCM practices are put into place, there are a number of available tools that aid in the ease and availability of information to effectively deploy the SCM efforts.

Another extremely important element that this book conveys is that there is a real and undeniable difference in SCM skill versus SCM power. Often, the largest original equipment manufacturers (OEMs) confuse the market power they exert over their suppliers with technical competency and skill. Power can be a blinding addiction, and only through the conversion to skill can sustainable improvements and positive supplier relationships be achieved. Chapter 3 specifically addresses this difference, and the rest of the book provides the direction and tools to develop the skill set.

Procurement efforts and procurement-based savings are the basis of this work. It is through the integration of the procurement efforts and supply chain management that the greatest and most sustained cost and profit improvements can be achieved. Supply chain management is a significantly varied and expanded discipline from logistics management. While logistics is a major element of SCM, it does not define SCM nor is it all encompassing of the SCM disciplines. SCM drives deeper into the value chain by which products and services are designed, developed, manufactured, purchased, and moved. Each of these elements and their contribution to total cost is part of our development of world class SCM.

THE CONTENTS AND STRUCTURE

Each of the major sections of the book has been organized to provide for an independent learning session. These sections have been created as stand-alone elements so that your organization can use the book and tools described, based upon where you are in development and maturity. An ongoing a case study within each chapter provides a glimpse into the successes and challenges in implementing the SCM practices. The case study company is a combination of a number of actual major tier-one automotive suppliers, and the implementation extends over a five-year period.

Section I — The Foundations. This section examines the organizational and cultural shift that must first take place to enable the use of lean tools, particularly within the supply chain organization. These changes create the environment in which an integrated SCM and company strategy can survive and flourish. Without these basics, many organizations will be unable to adequately address the need of the SCM and broader organization to ensure success of the SCM efforts.

Section II — The Crisis Environment. Section II examines the approaches and tools used when economic disaster is at hand. Various change concepts are introduced that link short-term economic focus with longer-term sustaining efforts. Driven by financial demands, these tools translate lean methods into specific actions focused on profit improvement. The key to this section is the development of the concept of short-term strategy, without losing focus on the broader and longer-term needs in an effort to meet short-term demands.

Section III — The Standard Environment. The third section provides the strategy and specific tools for an integrated SCM effort in a "normal" industry and economic environment. By their nature, the standard environment tools offered here are more deliberate, encompass a larger portion of the total SCM disciplines, and base the efforts on a more balanced approach to cost, quality, delivery, and technology (CQDT).

Section IV — Coordinating SCM and Lean Management. This final section can be used as part of the profile of the rest of the book, or as a stand-alone document regardless of the SCM strategies employed. The purpose of this section is to integrate the broader supply chain elements into the preparation for, and the success of, implementing lean manufacturing methods within your own company. The premise on which much of this book is based is derived from the author's personal experience, which is that SCM is an enabler of successful lean implementation. The SCM organization and its practices should not be treated as a stand-alone entity, but an extension of the rest of the organization.

ACKNOWLEDGEMENTS

As I finished the last page of the book, I looked back on the experience that made it all possible. I never would have made it this far without the help and inspiration of many great people.

Dave gave me the freedom to take as much rope as possible; Dennis showed me how to give it to others; and Donn showed me how not to hang myself — at least not fatally. My suppy chain teams did all the things I ever asked and developed truly world-class SCM organizations, proving many topics from the book. My dad, Ralph showed me how to develop a calm patience and allow good to happen, and not always try to force things.

SECTION I

The Foundations

1

The Purchasing/ SCM Executive as CEO

THE NUMBERS MAKE THE DIFFERENCE

Seasoned procurement professionals will tell you about the tremendous changes in their profession during the past 10 to 20 years. Among these changes have been the increased professional respect members of the purchasing profession have gained; the increase in the "arms length" transactions between the buyer and the seller, which is attributable to commercial relationships now being based on capabilities instead of personal relationships; and most important, the recognition by senior executives of the enormous contribution the supply chain management (SCM) organization can make to the company's bottom line.

The change in perception and behavior came hand in hand with the introduction of computer-based analysis tools, such as Lotus 1-2-3®, Microsoft Excel®. These tools began to shed light on the impact that material and supply chain savings could make to profit improvement. Figure 1.1 represents the composite of cost of goods breakdown for a typical tier-one automotive component supplier based on the experience of the author. These numbers are generally confirmed in many industry and procurement studies.

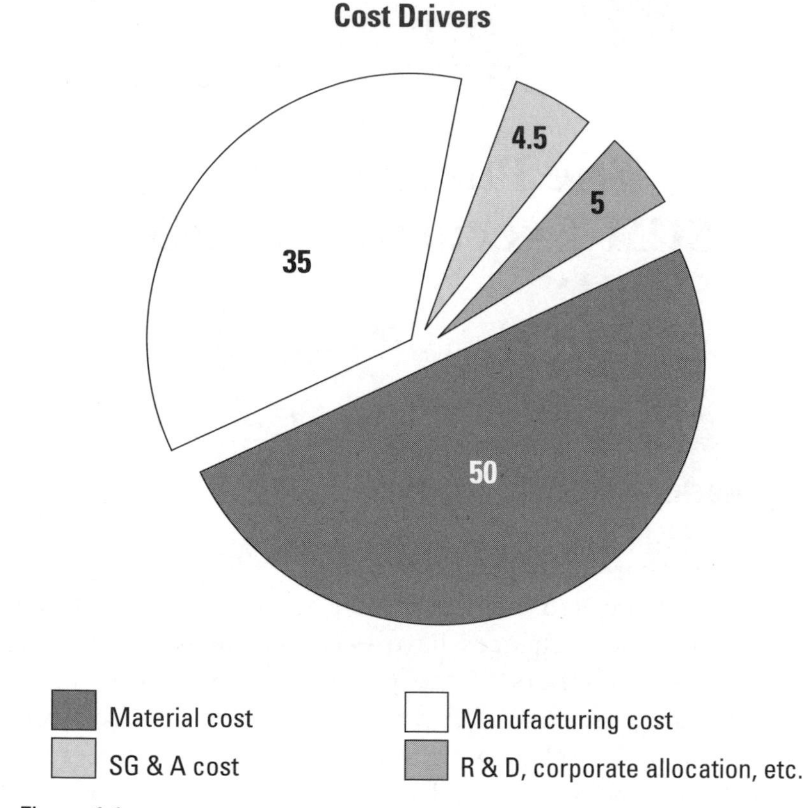

Figure 1.1

MORE THAN A COST CENTER

The fundamental mindset change that must be made is that procurement and supply chain organizations should not be treated as cost center support services, but as potential profit centers. This is possible only when executive management recognizes the potential profit contribution of strategic SCM and understands that the improvement potential of such an organization far outweighs its overhead costs. It is then that true strategic SCM can be effectively employed.

So how does an SCM organization transform from a cost center to a profit center? Very simply, the first step is to let the numbers

CASE STUDY 1.1

DSW Corporation (a fictional company based on composite experience) is a manufacturer of automotive electronics, safety, and body trim products. In 1995, DSW had seen its revenue grow by 15 to 20 percent for the prior two years and anticipated continued growth like this for the next three to four years based upon booked and likely anticipated sales. During the same period the annual gross profit had declined from 23 percent to 18 percent and annual pretax profit had declined from 5 percent to 3.25 percent. The forecast for the coming year GP and pretax were 17 percent and 2.75 percent. Many of DSW's customers were requiring annual price reductions of 3 to 5 percent, disallowing full recovery of prototype and development costs, and leveraging new competitors to determine price targets.

Organizationally, DSW had moved to a customer-focused sales and marketing activity, largely driven by the demands of its OEM customers. DSW's manufacturing, product development, and supply chain organizations were localized around individual product lines. DSW was evaluating the appropriate organizational structure to support the growth pattern and the need to maintain/improve profits.

Questions

1. What can DSW learn in managing its profits and SCM?
2. What changes in organization might aid the efforts that need to be taken?
3. What do the activities to date tell you about the focus of DSW?

speak for themselves. Table 1.1 shows the gross profit and pretax improvements that can be achieved for every dollar of sales with a 5 percent decrease in costs, or 5 percent increase in

Table 1.1 Cost and Profit Improvement

	Standard Price/Profit Model	5% Reduction in Material Content	5% Reduction in Manufacturing Cost	5% Increase in Sales
Sales	$1.00	$1.00	$1.00	$1.05
Material	($.50)	($.475)	($.50)	($.525)
Labor/OH	($.30)	($.30)	($.285)	($.315)
Gross Profit	$.20	$.225	$.215	$.21
Gross Profit Improvement		+ 12.5%	+ 7.5%	+ 5%
SG&A (Sales, General & Adminstrative Costs)	($.10)	($.10)	($.10)	($.105)
RD&E (Research, Design & Engineering Costs)	($.05)	($.05)	($.05)	($.0525)
Pretax Profit	$.05	$.075	$.065	$.0525
Profit Improvement		+ 50%	+ 30%	+ 5%

sales. The relationship between improved sales versus decreased material cost is about a 5:1 relationship at gross profit (see Table 1.2). Simply put, it takes $5 in increased sales to have the same profit effect as saving just $1 in material and supply chain costs.

The second way to transform the SCM organization is to recognize the relationship between the cost of the department to the total purchased dollars, or to the improvement contribution by the organization. Dave Nelson, in his book *Powered by Honda*,[1] discusses the value calculations that he used in determining the staffing level needed to support the strategic SCM efforts at Honda. Honda calculated that for every incremental dollar spent in supplier development (manpower resources), the organization was able to return $8 in cost improvement.[2] Generally, automotive-based procurement studies have pegged the total SCM SG&A budget at approximately 1½ percent to 2 percent of total purchased dollars. For the individual SCM contributor or employee, this means that there should be about a 8:1 payback to annual salary. It is this very measurable performance indicator that drives "CEO thinking" into the SCM organization. Many procurement and SCM organizations will target even higher payback levels, some up to 15 to 20 times annual salary.

MAKING THE SUPPLY CHAIN CEO

C. Ray Johnson in his book *CEO Logic*[3] discusses the idea of successful executive and functional managers thinking and acting like a CEO. His idea is that it is only by this "expansive" thinking that any executive is going to be able to understand the dependence and interdependency of their actions to the rest of the company, and ultimately to the company's profitability.

1. Dave Nelson, Patricia E. Moody, and Rick Mayo, *Powered by Honda: Developing Excellence in the Global Enterprise* (New York: John Wiley & Sons, 1998).
2. Nelson et al, *Powered by Honda*, p. 205.
3. C. Ray Johnson, *CEO Logic: How to Think and Act Like a Chief Executive* (Franklin Lakes, NJ: Career Press, 1998).

Table 1.2 Profit Improvement Per $1 Sales Increase or Material Decrease

Change per $100 in sales	Standard Price/ Profit Model	$1 Decrease to Material Content	$1 Increase in Sales
Sales	$100	$100	$101
Material	($50)	($ 49)	($ 50.5)
Labor/OH	($30)	($ 30)	($ 30.3)
Gross Profit	$ 20	$ 21	$ 20.2
Gross Profit Improvement		+ 5%	+ 1%
SG&A	($ 10)	($ 10)	($ 10.1)
RD&E	($ 5)	($ 5)	($ 5.05)
Pretax Profit	$ 5	$ 6	$ 5.05
Profit Improvement		+ 20%	+ 1%

He lists the necessary thoughts and attributes of the budding "CEO," and how his or her own area of responsibility can achieve its greatest success.

Among Johnson's lists of actions is to focus on the customer.[4] The main reason for this is obvious, sales equals product and product equals profit. Although SCM executives should consider the ultimate product buyers to be their customers, internal customers are more likely to be their focus. Using the CEO idea, SCM executives can integrate their strategies into the broader needs of the organization, be more certain of focusing on the critical needs of the company, ensure broader support of their efforts, and be able to clearly articulate SCM's success and contribution to the organization. Examples of this integration are demonstrated throughout this book, especially in the discussion on performance, strategic SCM plans, and, finally, in the launch of lean systems.

This book also discusses the importance of tracking key performance measures and the role they play in determining the success of the supply chain organization. Here especially, the procurement or supply chain executive must transcend the normal view of performance and think like a CEO. A key measure that the CEO looks at is earnings per share (EPS), and often this single measure determines the success or failure of the CEO. Likewise, the supply chain executive must also translate the contribution of his activities to EPS. Figure 1.2 shows the method by which DSW translated its hard cost supply chain savings to EPS. DSW was a publicly traded company with 25,000,000 fully diluted outstanding shares of stock.

Reflecting the savings in this manner is necessary to fully understand the broad contribution that the SCM organization is making to the company. The growth in gross savings and EPS

---

4. C. Ray Johnson, *CEO Logic.*

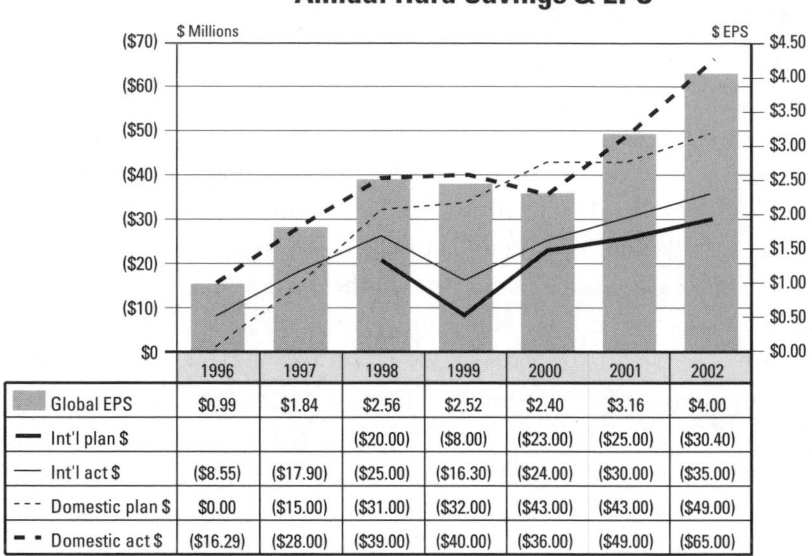

	1996	1997	1998	1999	2000	2001	2002
Global EPS	$0.99	$1.84	$2.56	$2.52	$2.40	$3.16	$4.00
Int'l plan $			($20.00)	($8.00)	($23.00)	($25.00)	($30.40)
Int'l act $	($8.55)	($17.90)	($25.00)	($16.30)	($24.00)	($30.00)	($35.00)
Domestic plan $	$0.00	($15.00)	($31.00)	($32.00)	($43.00)	($43.00)	($49.00)
Domestic act $	($16.29)	($28.00)	($39.00)	($40.00)	($36.00)	($49.00)	($65.00)

Figure 1.2 DSW Corporation "Hard" SCM Savings & EPS Contribution

contribution demonstrated by DSW's SCM organization reflects the various steps taken in creating a lean supply chain and those that are the basis of this book. It is through the practices outlined in this book that actual and significant savings can be made. For example, in Figure 1.2, the savings obtained in the "international plan" and "international actual" were largely obtained through the tools and practices described in the Crisis Environment section outlined in Chapters 4 through 9. The savings listed under the "domestic plan" and "domestic actual" represent savings achieved using the tools described in the Standard Environment section in Chapters 10 through 15.

CASE STUDY 1.2

Questions

1. What can DSW learn in managing its profits and SCM?
2. What changes in organization might aid the efforts that need to be taken?
3. What do the activities to date tell you about the focus of DSW?

Answers

1. DSW recognized the importance that SCM played as a percentage of its total cost of goods sold. In the case of DSW, SCM content represented approximately 60 percent of total COGS. The historic performance of SCM savings was very small, thus enabling some immediate identification of improvements which could be undertaken. Based on its cost and balance sheet structure, for every $1 saving in SCM savings, approximately $.85–$.90 flowed to the pretax level. Additionally however, the reduction in material assets reduced the property tax liability as well, so in some cases the pretax effect may have been greater than $1 to $1 at pretax.
2. The SCM organization at DSW stepped through three distinct steps. The first was the integration of a single domestic SCM organization responsible for all aspects of SCM. In the case of DSW, this included procurement, supplier development, traffic and transportation, and distribution. The second step was the integration of a single international SCM organization responsible for managing the

Continued on next page

company's non-North American SCM needs. The final step was the integration of these two regional groups into a single global activity.

3. Like many of the other companies in this industry, DSW's activities reflected the focus on sales/marketing and new product development. While these are undoubtedly critical elements is business survival and growth, the benefits achieved were not sufficient to sustain the profitability but only revenue growth. This is a very typical situation in this industry.

2

The Disciplines of Planning

IDENTIFICATION OF OVERARCHING OBJECTIVES

The first step in the implementation of lean SCM practices is the identification of the needs and objectives for which these activities will occur. To ensure that there is a method behind the madness, or at least an objective behind the action, the clear identification of the ends support the means by which we are going to arrive. Without these end markers in mind, SCM and lean manufacturing (and anything else) ring hollow with the "flavor of the month" feel. The team members within an organization are unable to rally around the activity because they often do not understand the purpose of the activity, the activity itself, or the value in the new approach versus the current methods.

Of the many planning approaches that exist in business today, management by planning (MBP),[1] or hoshin planning, is unparalleled in its ability to articulate the objectives to be delivered, the plans by which the objectives will be delivered, the ownership of the team in delivering the objectives, and management's

1. "Management by Planning" was first used by Intel, *Setting The Direction: Management by Planning*, Catherine Johnston and Mark Daniel, 1993.

CASE STUDY 2.1

DSW concluded its annual planning process as it did every year, right on time—1½ months after the start of the fiscal year. Included in its annual performance goals was to achieve an increase in pretax profits by 15 percent, to reduce total costs by 10 percent, increase sales by 15 percent, and improve customer performance by 25 percent.

As the organization was put to work to implement these goals, there was an undercurrent of confusion. Not necessarily confusion over the goals themselves, but confusion in how these goals were any different than the goals of the past three years. Over the past three years the goals had been largely the same, and in all the past three years the goals were never met. There always seemed to be a mismatch between the desired outcomes and those by which individual performance was measured.

Questions

1. How was the executive management at DSW going to "institutionalize" the goals and their attainment for the new fiscal year?
2. Where in the goal setting process did DSW need to bring in its team members to ensure achievement of the goals?
3. What does DSW need to recognize as the most important element(s) in actually meeting the new fiscal year goals?

responsibility in aiding the team in meeting these objectives (see Figure 2.1). In Michael Cowley and Ellen Domb's book, *Beyond Strategic Vision: Effective Corporate Action with Hoshin Planning*, the authors articulate the clear differences between MBP and operational or strategic planning.

Operational planning typically focuses on short-term (less than one year) and financial measures, and strategic planning typically focuses on only the broadest issues.[2] The failure of both operational and most strategic planning lies in the fact that the plan becomes more important than the planning process. This is the downfall of "management by objective" (MBO). In MBO, the stated objective becomes the focus and not the process by which the objective is achieved. By contrast, in MPB the goal is to become a learning organization through the activity of planning and the implementation of these plans. As Cowley and Domb state, MBP (hoshin) is really the application of the plan-do-check-act (PDCA) cycle to business activities.[3]

Applying MBP to the integration of lean SCM and activities first involves identifying common overarching objectives. Overarching objectives simply are the highest-level objectives based directly on the strategic intent of the company. These objectives are stated in ways such as: "Increase shareholder value by x percent per year," or "Improve customer quality levels from x to y," or "Improve employee satisfaction index from y to z." These overarching objectives are often set by identifying the few key strategies and expressing them as a simple phrase or shared logo. For example, Hewlett-Packard's core businesses are measurement, computation, and communication. Its MPB overarching objectives are centered on this "HP=MC^2" theme.[4]

SCM and lean manufacturing intersect most significantly in profitability objectives, customer satisfaction objectives, and quality objectives. It is typically these three areas and the resulting strategic activities that drive the coordinated operational actions.

2. Micheal Cowley and Ellen Domb 1997, *Beyond Strategic Vision: Effective Corporate Action with Hoshin Planning* (Burlington, MA: Butterworth-Heinemann, 1997), p. 3.
3. Cowley & Domb, *Beyond Strategic Vision*, p. 5.
4. Cowley & Domb, *Beyond Strategic Vision*. p. 20.

Failures of Traditional Planning Activities	Advantages of MBP
Forecasts are unrealistic and no process exists to recognize gaps and adjust plan.	Organizational objectives arise from the company's strategic vision.
Arbitrary objectives are often set without consideration to "need, means or feasibility" of achieving goal.	Specific methodologies exist to define "breakthrough" actions on the key objectives.
There are often too many goals to focus on the "high-leverage" or high-impact items.	All activities occurring in the organization are focused around the "overarching" objectives.
Incorrect goals are often set, and there is no process to link goals to activities.	All levels of the organization feel "ownership" of the activities and the objectives.
"There is no shared vision of the organization's future," and therefore to ownership of plans.	The implementation system is extremely firm and flexible at the same time.
The ongoing activities are not based on achieving the goals, causing the goals to become a "wish list."	A "supportive review system" exists, which allows correction to the plan during the action implementation.
Ongoing reviews of activities do not occur to evaluate progress toward goals.	The process is based upon learning and ongoing correction or is described as "adaptive and self-healing."
Where review of goal attainment occurs, the punitive nature of the review causes a "CYA" approach.	
Because management has not mastered effective planning, past failures inhibit future planning.	
Planning teams do not understand the difference between operational planning and strategic planning.	
The plan is the goal, not the planning (and learning) process.	
Objective measures and factual data often do not exist during the planning cycle OR the converse— planning suffers analysis paralysis.	
Planning departments and not the functional managers do the planning.	

Figure 2.1 Planning Method Comparison

Finally, as the basis of MBP, the overarching objectives are defined by the senior management team and are based upon stakeholder needs. Depending upon the company culture, the stakeholders may be any or all of its shareholders, customers, employees, suppliers, community members, or others. By basing the strategic intent and overarching objectives on the shareholder needs, all the effected constituents will be considered in the daily activities of the organization.

DEVELOPMENT OF STRATEGIC PLANS AND ACTIONS

These highest-level overarching objectives need to be distilled to real life activities and goals. The typical focus at this point becomes financially-based operational plans. Financial measures alone, however, are not sufficient to prepare the organization for the work to follow, especially keeping in mind that one of the premises of MBP is that learning from the planning and implementation process is as important as the plan itself. Focusing only on financial objectives limits the organization from making critical changes. The concept of strategic learning suggests that the companies that are the most successful in the broadest terms have mastered strategic thinking versus strategic planning.[5]

To appropriately define a balanced mix of financial and nonfinancial measures, the use of a Balanced Scorecard[6] is recommended. The *Harvard Business Review* describes the methods

---

5. Henry Mintzberg, The Rise and Fall of Strategic Planning (New York: Free Press, Macmillan, 1994), p. 209–210
6. Robert Kaplin & David Norton, "The Balanced Scorecard–Measures that Drive Performance," *Harvard Business Review*, January–February 1992, pp. 72. Author's note: Since the 1992 HBR article, Kaplan & Norton have expanded balanced scorecard theory to a management system (*Harvard Business Review* January–February 1996 which is essentially the adoption of management by planning (hoshin) practices.

and advantages by which the balanced measures can be selected. These balanced objectives support the overarching goals arising from the MBP process. Using an MPB tool called a goals and action (G&A) matrix,[7] SCM and manufacturing operations managers can clearly articulate their objectives with reference to the overarching goals. The G&A matrix also allows the alignment of potentially conflicting objectives. For example, an SCM objective may be to reduce inbound transportation costs while a manufacturing objective may be to improve inventory turns or increase delivery frequency; the SCM goal would pursue *decreased* delivery frequency while the manufacturing goal would pursue *increased* delivery frequency. The development of the G&A goals, and the supportive reviews of the activity progress highlight such conflicts.

Formatting the strategic intent, highest-level objectives, and second-level (functional or departmental) goals are more an extension of the existing business than a change to a new way of operating. In a learning organization, it is critical to take the best of the current practices into future plans. However, it is out of the existing failures or obstacles that plans for change are developed. Earlier we discussed the potential failure of the planning process through the lack of ownership of the new direction by all levels of the organization. To rally all levels of the organization around the new direction, the shared vision must be flowed from level to level. This can be most effectively done through a process called catchball, which is discussed in the following section.

IMPLEMENTATION PLANS AND TASK IDENTIFICATION

So now the senior management team has identified a strategic direction and intent for the company and the highest-level

---

7. Jeffrey Wincel, "A Practitioners View of Strategic Procurement," *Supply Chain Management Review.* (Summer 1998), p. 63, exhibit 4.

goals have been set, but how does the rank and file worker gain the vision? How do work teams at all levels of the organization gain the vision? Catchball is the collaboration method where the work strategies are selected by understanding the strategic vision and objectives.[8] The work team leader first tosses the ball (the ideas) to his team members by articulating the overarching objectives and the team-level (department) goals associated with the overarching objectives. Where there is uncertainty or needed amplification, the team tosses the ball back to the team leader. This process continues until there is extreme clarity of the strategic intent and the specific work elements that will drive toward that intent. Every team member fully understands exactly how their daily work is related to the team goal, the overarching goal, and strategic intent, ultimately for the satisfaction of the stakeholders. (See Figure 2.2.)

In this analysis, tightly coordinated work activities are necessary to deliver the optimal outcomes for lean manufacturing and SCM. Tasks that occur at the most basic levels must be outlined in a way in which there is no misunderstanding as to who will be doing what. This clear-cut job definition is especially important in activities with shared or cross-functional responsibilities. The primary interface between supply management and manufacturing operations in a lean environment is materials management responsibilities. Where manufacturing material handling will be looking for material flow improvements, procurement must ensure that the supply base is prepared to support the operational needs in significantly different ways (which is discussed in greater detail in a later chapter). The entire supplier management (and where necessary supplier development) issue is often overlooked as each group assumes the other responsible. The responsibility matrix in Figure 2.3 is an example of the clear definition of multigroup interface and ownership.

---

8. Cowley & Domb, *Beyond Strategic Vision.* pp. 28–29.

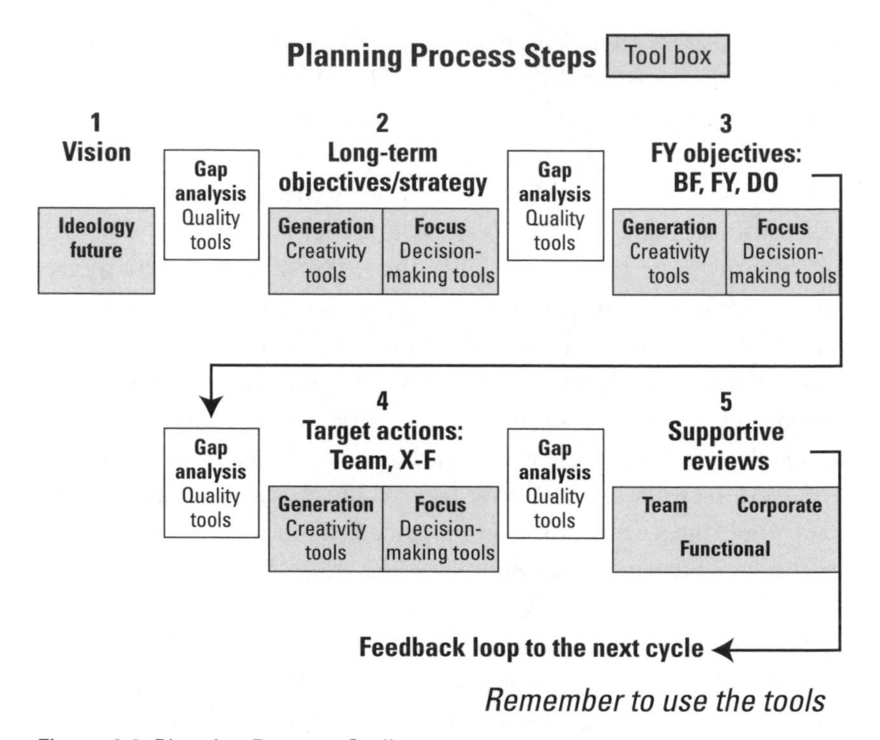

Figure 2.2 Planning Process Outline (2002 Magna Donnelly Corporation w/ permission)

Specific work elements and processes to be followed exist in each area of responsibility. This matrix does not detail those work elements, but identifies the person or activity responsible for delivering the action for the shared work. While this example is not a shared SCM lean manufacturing work element, it does exemplify a cross-functional responsibility affecting supply management, manufacturing, and program management.

Finally, regular supportive reviews by the senior management team must be an ongoing part of the process. It is through these reviews that the implementers are able to examine their activities, learn from the progress, and adapt as necessary. Managers are able to verify that the shared vision is really shared at all levels, and that the actions the organization is taking are in support of the highest-level objectives. Adopting lean manufactur-

Responsibility Matrix—Launch Review	Plant quality / AQE	Tactical supplier quality engineer	Program team	Strategic SQE	Supplier quality management
Areas of concern					
LRR (launch readiness review) responsibility					
Develop LRR Process	□	□		●	□
Define individual module components for LRR	▼	▼	●		
Establish target date for LRR (derived from APQP)	▼	▼	●		
Communicate expectations to supplier		●			□
Schedule LRR at supplier's location	▼	▼			
Conduct LRR at supplier's location	▼	●	□	□	
Communicate review findings to appropriate parties	▼	●			
Follow-up and close-out open issues as a result of review findings	▼	▼	▼	□	□

● Lead
▼ Support
□ Resource

Figure 2.3 Responsibility Matrix

ing disciplines can be among the most difficult activities a company can undergo. Managing them concurrently with the implementation of advanced supply chain techniques requires even more attention. The supportive review process aids in all of this by identifying the factors that inhibit forward momentum and works to quickly eliminate them. If the management team can't break down the barriers, no one will be able to.

TRANSLATING THE OBJECTIVES TO THE PLAN

Translating the objectives into a plan is the single objective of MBP or hoshin planning (often called *hoshin kanri*). Hoshin planning by its definition is policy deployment. In fact, Womak and Jones in their book *Lean Thinking* define hoshin as "a strategic decision-making tool for a firm's executive team that focuses resources on the critical initiatives necessary to accomplish the business objectives of the firm."[9]

The methodology generally recommended to translate and deploy the overarching objectives is a visual method similar to quality functional deployment.[10] Sometimes called a "goals and action matrix," this format represents the cascade of the select few key measures to department objectives to individual work tasks. Figure 2.4 represents a supply chain G&A matrix, including procurement, supplier quality, process, etc.

The highest-level overarching objectives must first be strategically selected by the executive management team and represent the increases or improvements in value as perceived by the customer. These are often defined as a mixture of product customer demands, but more often as constituent demands of which customers are one. The need to differentiate between customers and constituents is driven by the reality of business. In most real world environments, businesses have to answer to all of their constituents—that is, their customers, shareholders or lenders, employees, and others—not just to the people or organizations who buy their products. Executive management must define the objectives with which improved or increased value can be delivered to these constituents.

Figure 2.5 shows the right side of the G&A matrix in which the overarching objectives are identified. These objectives should address each of the constituents as well as business fundamentals.

This example demonstrates objectives aligned with stakeholder or constituent needs. For example, objectives 1 & 2 are directly related to shareholder requirements; objectives 3 & 4 are cus-

---

9. James P. Womack and Daniel T. Jones, *Lean Thinking: Banish Waste and Create Weath in Your Corporation* (New York: Simon & Schuster, 1996), p. 306.
10. Womak & Jones, *Lean Thinking*, p. 307.

Goals and Action Matrix—FY

Team: Corporate Materials | **Leader:**

9 100% implementation of ISO 14000	8 50% improvement of supplier delivery to 8500 PPM	7 50% improvement of supplier quality to 1200 PPM	6 50% national average for lost work incidents	5 55th percentile on system 5 climate rating	4 50% reduction to 600 short ships	3 50% reduction in CPPM to 161	2 15% compounded growth in sales	1 RDA of 6%		Fiscal Year Objectives			1 Certify tooling suppliers	2 Develop procurement and card pilot program	3 Ship direct from manufacturing	4 Improve inventory accuracy	5 Improve PPAP approval	6 Increase suppliers % QS9000 certification	7 Achieve LRR's 100%	8 Increase minority supply base	9 Increase LTAs	10 Reduce supply base
						X		X	8	FY	Implement procurement card program				X		X					
								X	7	FY	Reduce freight as a % to purchase receipts	15%									X	X
						X			6	FY	Zero CAR's past due—QS9000 audits						X	X	X			
								X	5	FY	Achieve annual plan budget										X	X
				X					4	FY	55th percentile on system 5 climate ratings	75%										
					X		X	X	3	FY	50% reduction in supplier delivery to 8500 PPM	60%	X			X	X		X		X	X
						X	X	X	2	FY	50% reduction in supplier quality to 1200 PPM	60%				X	X	X	X		X	X
								X	1	FY	Achieve PPV of 2% savings (less customer glass)	3%	X	X		X	X		X		X	X
											Material fiscal year objectives	OS										

Materials team—Leader:

Management by planning

Target champion

Figure 2.4 A Supply Chain Goals and Action Matrix

9	100% implementation of ISO 14000	
8	50% improvement of supplier delivery to 8500 PPM	
7	50% improvement of supplier quality to 1200 PPM	
6	50% national average for lost work incidents	
5	55th percentile on system 5 climate rating	
4	50% reduction to 600 short ships	
3	50% reduction in CPPM to 161	
2	15% compounded growth in sales	
1	RDA of 6%	
	NAAO Fiscal Year Objectives	

Figure 2.5 G & A Matrix Overarching Objectives

Goals and Action Matrix—FY

Materials

	X	8	FY	Implement procurement card program		
	X	7	FY	Reduce freight as a % to purchase receipts	15%	
		6	FY	Zero CAR's past due—QS9000 audits		
	X	5	FY	Achieve annual plan budget		
		4	FY	55th percentile on system 5 climate ratings	75%	
X	X	3	FY	50% reduction in supplier delivery to 8500 PPM	60%	
X	X	2	FY	50% reduction in supplier quality to 1200 PPM	60%	
	X	1	FY	Achieve PPV of 2% savings (less customer glass)	3%	
				Material fiscal year objectives	OS	

Figure 2.6 G & A Matrix Department Objectives

tomer value objectives, in this case quality and satisfaction requirements; objectives 5 & 6 are employee based; objectives 7 & 8 are supplier related; and 9 is interpreted here as serving the community constituent.

Figure 2.6 translates the overarching objectives into departmental objectives. The "x's" on the left upper side of the matrix represent where the overarching objectives are being supported by the departmental objectives. It is at this intersection where you can begin to see the purpose of individual department efforts, why they are being put in place, and what their broader purpose is. It is also here that the first series of catchball activities occur. The translation of the overarching objectives to workable organizational objectives is a critical element in understanding the purpose and ingrained philosophy by which the company will be run. Lean concepts are an example of the philosophy.

Also present in the matrix is an "OS" column that represents outstanding performance. The outstanding performance can be represented as some percentage increase over the baseline plan. This is often 25 percent or more and may represent levels possible with *kaikaku. Kaikaku* is radical change efforts that will be discussed later. Where incentives play a role in managerial compensation, it should be these objectives and stretch objectives that are the basis for the incentive payouts.

Finally, the right side of the matrix (Figure 2.7) represents the translation of the departmental objectives to individual actions. Again, catchball plays a big role in being certain that the individual tasks and support of the departmental objectives are clearly understood. The upper right "x's" show the intersection of the individual actions to the departmental objectives. Through these intersections, individuals can see how their daily efforts support the highest-level objectives, objectives that may have previously been hard to communicate.

1	Certify tooling suppliers		X		X
2	Develop procurement and card pilot program		X		
3	Ship direct from manufacturing				
4	Improve inventory accuracy		X	X	X
5	Improve PPAP approval		X	X	X
6	Increase suppliers % QS9000 certification			X	
7	Achieve LRR's 100%		X	X	X
8	Increase minority supply base				
9	Increase LTAs		X	X	X
10	Reduce supply base		X	X	X

Figure 2.7 G & A Matrix Individual Actions

MONITORING THE PROGRESS OF THE PLAN

Although knowing how to link individual actions to departmental objectives and ultimately to overarching objectives is extremely important, it has no value if you are unable to achieve results. Historically, annual objectives were rolled out, implemented, and then put away until the next planning or review cycle a year later. Not much was done in the way of actually understanding how well planned actions were being implemented. If midyear reviews did take place, it normally was an unpleasant dressing down.

MBP implementation varies significantly in that regular reviews are part of the process—again reflecting the idea that the process is just as important as the plan itself. These supportive reviews reflect the idea that the individual actions are critical to the overarching objectives, and provide for the allocation or

Key Measure and Target Activity Summary

Date:

Achieve PPV of 2% savings

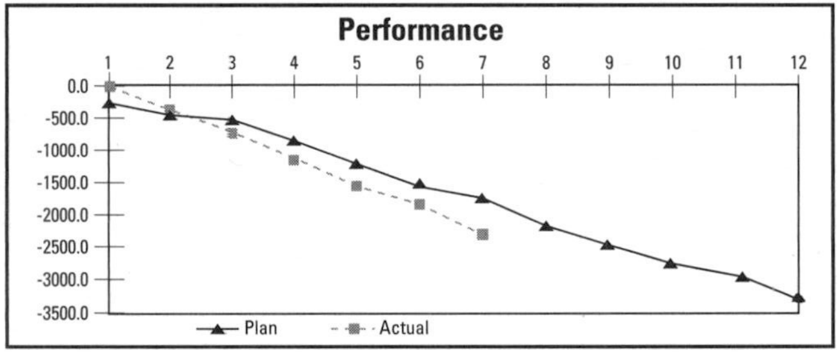
Performance
0.0
-500.0
-1000.0
-1500.0
-2000.0
-2500.0
-3000.0
-3500.0
1
2
3
4
5
6
7
8
9
10
11
12
Plan
Actual

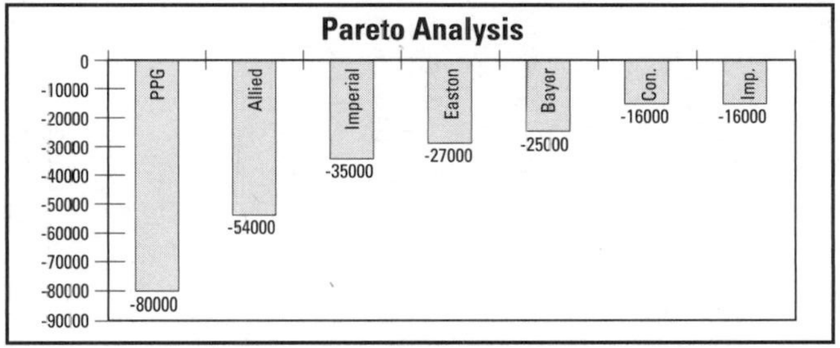
Pareto Analysis
0
-10000
-20000
-30000
-40000
-50000
-60000
-70000
-80000
-90000
PPG
-80000
Allied
-54000
Imperial
-35000
Easton
-27000
Bayer
-25000
Con.
-16000
Imp.
-16000

	1997 Actual	1998 Actual	1999 Plan	OS
Actual	1.6M	2.8M	-2339.7	<--YTD
Plan YTD			-1653.6	

	July	Aug	Sept	Oct	Nov	Dec	Jan	Feb	Mar	April	June	July
Actual	-104.5	-457.0	-860.7	-1283.7	-1610.8	-1819.8	-2339.7	0.0	0.0	0.0	0.0	0.0
Plan	-217.2	-434.4	-651.6	-323.1	-1194.6	-1394.6	-1653.6	-2009.1	-2280.6	-2606.6	-2932.6	-3258.6

Actual to plan
Performances
ABOVE PLAN

Increases	Cause	Corrective Action	Who	When
Supplier A	Paint	Build out - May	Buyer 1	May 200X
Supplier B	Change in paint requirements	Change standards - RTS/EO	Buyer 2	Feb 200X
Supplier C	Smaller order quantities - pics	Review pricing schedule	Buyer 3	Feb 200X
Supplier D	Yen fluctuation	None - current contact adjustment	Buyer 1	
Supplier E	Incorrect standards	Change incorrect standards	Buyer 4	Feb 200X
Supplier F	Coil spring - take it/leave it	None	Buyer 2	
Supplier G	Incorrect standards	Change incorrect standards	Buyer 2	Oct 200X

Figure 2.8 Action Performance Summary Chart

reallocation of the necessary assets, or to break roadblocks to allow for the successful accomplishment of the goals. Again from *Lean Thinking*,[11] the performance monitoring aspect of MBP unifies and aligns resources and establishes clearly measurable targets against which progress toward the key objectives is measured on a regular basis." While there are many methods for measuring progress, Figure 2.8[12] shows a method by which each of the key objectives are tracked for monthly performance, year-to-date performance, pareto of reasons for success or failure, gap analysis with actions, and responsible individuals with target completion dates. Through the incorporated use of radar

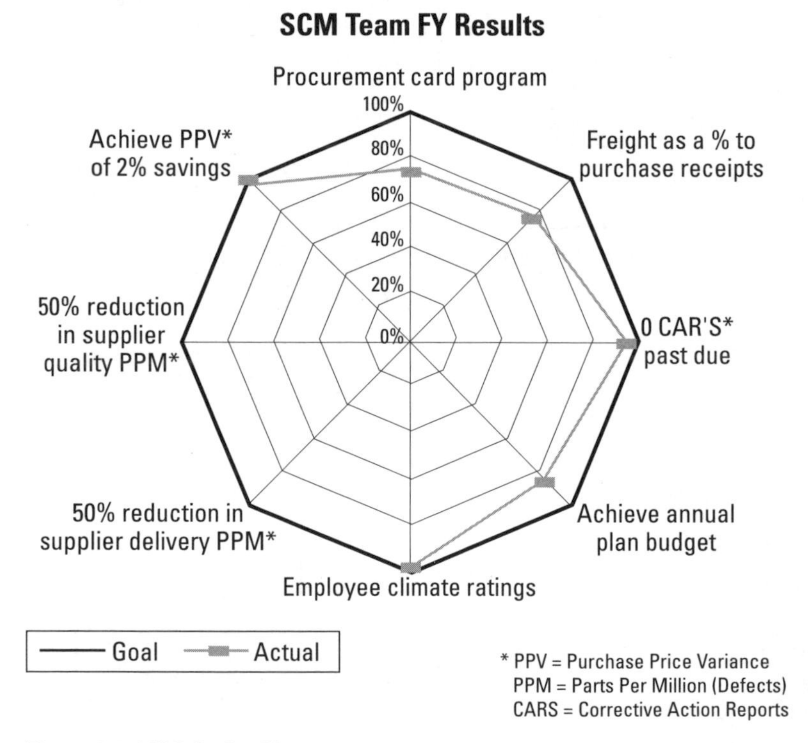

Figure 2.9 MBP Radar Chart

11. Womak & Jones, *Lean Thinking*, p. 307.
12. Used with permission Magna Donnelly Corporation, 1999.

charts, management can quickly identify those areas that require review and those where progress is on target (Figure 2.9).

CASE STUDY 2.2

Questions

1. How was the executive management at DSW going to "institutionalize" the goals and their attainment for the new fiscal year?
2. Where in the goal setting process did DSW need to bring in its team members to ensure achievement of the goals?
3. What does DSW need to recognize as the most important element(s) in actually meeting the new fiscal year goals?

Answers

1. The goals were institutionalized by the development of "Overarching Objectives" designed to address the expressed needs of the various "stakeholders."
2. DSW brought in the team members in the setting of the department level goals. These goals were set based upon support and achieving the over-arching objectives.
3. There were a number of "most important factors" with some of those being: i) making available the tools and resources needed to support the individual and departmental objectives; ii) the use of executive level supportive reviews to break any obstacles in achieving goals; and iii) directly tying team and personal goals to the business plan objectives for performance evaluations.

3

Force Versus Skill

Supply chain organizations often have their business style driven by pressures from other parts of the organization or by other players in their industry. The form in which SCM professionals interact with the supply base is one of the clearest examples of how company vision and business ethics translate to daily behavior and professional performance. Each business method has a greatly varying impact on supplier relationships and performance. While the ultimate objectives of achieving improvements in cost, quality, and other business indicators may be similar, the sustainability of these improvements and their impact on suppliers have very different effects.

This chapter examines the effects of buyer-supplier relationships and proposes a rediscovery of business ethics and corporate morality. In defining buy-sell relationships beyond a traditional view, the foundations of SCM improvements that are made possible by the tools defined throughout the book are put into place. Without a philosophical basis on which to build supplier relationships, these tools simply become another collection of initiatives, and not a bolder business strategy.

CASE STUDY 3.1

DSW had finalized its participation in an online auction for its major customer, which should result in the awarding of $45 million in annual sourcing for a major new program. This sourcing should happen because DSW won the competitive auction for price, delivery, tooling, and productivity terms (annual price downs). The uncertainty is simply a built in part of OEM sourcing process.

Although DSW was winning on all the key requirements of the sourcing package, at the source confirmation meeting there was one final requirement. DSW was given the opportunity to secure the business, provided they further reduced the current price of an unrelated, current production part beyond the contract committed rate. By increasing the annual price reduction from 4 percent to 6.5 percent, DSW would receive the new business.

Questions:

1. How should DSW respond to its customer with respect to the sourcing proposal considering that the current part was sourcing with 18 percent gross profit and 3.5 percent pretax, and was two years into a four-year contract with 4 percent annual price reductions; and that the new part was quoted at 17 percent and 3 percent profits rates and 3.5 percent annual price reductions?
2. To meet the annual customer price reductions, what can DSW do to reduce its cost structure?
3. What does DSW's customer's purchasing organization believe about its ability to negotiate the new product sourcing and potentially achieve incremental reduction on existing business?

THE "BOY, I'M GOOD" SYNDROME

The typical profile of a new production buyer at the automotive original equipment manufacturers (OEMs) is a high-flying MBA. They are selected based on their ability to understand the complexities of cost and profit structures and their desire to make a mark in the organization and progress rapidly, and also because of the regular availability of a new class of employees. These characteristics serve the OEMs well by providing the critical analysis skills and aggressiveness in dealing with sourcing issues. The mix of skill and desire create a competitive attitude in which winning becomes the main goal.

Training and development is provided as a regular part of the orientation of the new buyers. Included with that training is the idea of partnerships and win-win. These concepts are designed to eliminate the confrontational nature of the buy-sell relationship. Novice and seasoned buyers alike believe that they exercise the concepts of fairness with their suppliers as they negotiate and source business. The achievements they make in negotiated cost reductions, sourcing below target, and achieving annual improvements are made in the context of training, experience, and partnership perspectives. Obviously, the buyers must be good to get these improvements, creating the "boy, I must be good" belief.

IS THE PLAYING FIELD LEVEL?

Success is based on achieving winning results by understanding the rules of the game, playing better than the competition, and getting the outcome you desire. In the sourcing activities of SCM, the rules seemed to change often—at least in the automotive world. More often than not, the rules in the buy-sell relationship are solely determined by the biggest guy on the block (the guy with the most leverage)—usually the OEM customer. Often the OEMs either don't recognize the reality of this playing field tilt, or they don't admit to it.

Figure 3.1 demonstrates the effects on profitability in a buy-sell relationship between a major tier-one supplier and one of its biggest customers. Because of confidentiality reasons, the companies can't be identified, but the information is taken from publicly available data. The data shows a seemingly direct correlation between the average annual part price reductions, the increase in the customer's pretax profits, and a corresponding decline in the supplier's pretax profits. While the supplier's reductions individually do not represent the increase in the customer's pretax profits, it does reflect the average reductions given across the entire supply base.

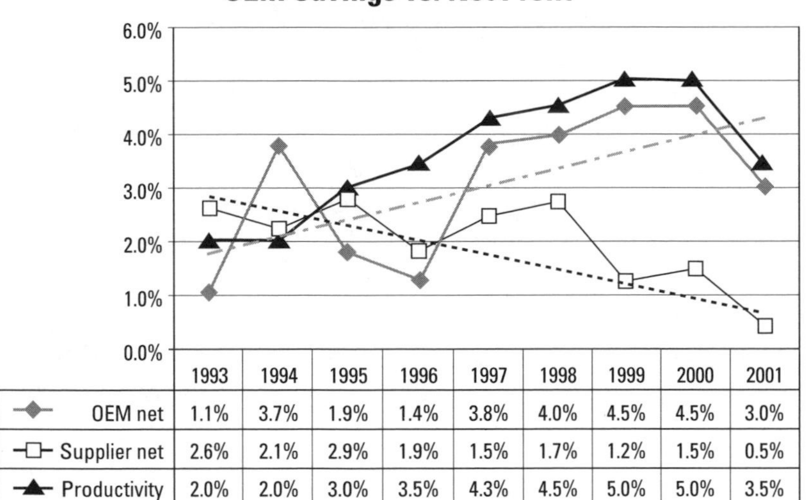

	1993	1994	1995	1996	1997	1998	1999	2000	2001
OEM net	1.1%	3.7%	1.9%	1.4%	3.8%	4.0%	4.5%	4.5%	3.0%
Supplier net	2.6%	2.1%	2.9%	1.9%	1.5%	1.7%	1.2%	1.5%	0.5%
Productivity	2.0%	2.0%	3.0%	3.5%	4.3%	4.5%	5.0%	5.0%	3.5%

Figure 3.1

THE ETHICS OF BUSINESS

Generally, the companies who have embraced and implemented lean methodologies try to model themselves after the example of the Toyota Production System (TPS). One of the hallmark features of the lean methods of TPS is that there exists an underlying philosophy that guides individual practices and efforts—that is, clearly defined ethics drive behavior. It is the critical nature of these business ethics that enables the successful implementation and ongoing success of lean practices.

The drive to win in the supply chain relationship determines the behavior exhibited by the SCM professionals. SCM professionals in North America generally believe that the tactics they employ are not only ethical, but positively contribute to the buy-sell relationships. The way to validate the truth in that belief is to examine the individual behaviors and their impact on relationship building. By moving from destructive to constructive behaviors, the ethical and philosophical backbone of the SCM strategy can be established, enabling a positive win strategy.

Dr. David R. Hawkins, in his book *Power vs. Force—The Hidden Determinants of Human Behavior*, describes the effects of these two methods of influencing others on personal, professional, and commercial relationships. Dr. Hawkins writes that "power arises from meaning. It has to do with motive, and it has to do with principal."[1] In contrast to the positive aspects of ethics in power, force depends on the lowest basic behaviors, appealing to crass influence actions.[2] Like Isaac Newton's law of physics, forces in commercial relationships have a counterforce fighting against them, whereas positive power derived from ethical behavior "energizes, gives forth, supplies, and supports."[3] So the determining factors the SCM professionals need to examine in evaluating the ethics by which they interact professionally are the behaviors they exhibit.

1. David R. Hawkins, M.D., Ph.D., *Power vs. Force: The Hidden Determinants of Human Behavior* (Carlsbad, CA.: Hay House Inc., 1995), p. 132.
2. Hawkins, *Power vs. Force*, pp. 132–134.
3. Hawkins, *Power vs. Force*, pp. 132–134.

WHERE POWER (SKILL) IS DERIVED

Dr. Hawkins describes strong and weak behaviors that influence relationships.[4] The following list represents a small sampling simply to allow readers to assess their behavior and ethics in professional SCM:

- Authoritative/dogmatic.
- Aware/preoccupied.
- Candid/calculating.
- Conciliatory/inflexible.
- Confident/arrogant.
- Defending/attacking.
- Diplomatic/deceptive.
- Equal/superior.
- Ethical/equivocal.
- Honest/legal.
- Ingenious/scheming.
- Leading/coercive.
- Observant/suspicious.
- Powerful/forceful.
- Requesting/demanding.
- Valuing/exploitive.

The first word in each pair represents the positive power characteristic. The second represents the force characteristic. Exhibiting behaviors reflective of the first of these pairs leads to the ethical basis and underlying philosophy that will deliver the greatest possible success in implementing lean SCM.

The transition from force to skill is based on learning. This is not necessarily learning in the educational seminar sense, but

4. Hawkins, *Power vs. Force*, pp. 145–147.

learning in the experiential sense, especially on the losing side. Educational learning provides a set of finite tools that can be employed as techniques. Typically these tools are used as part of a game plan to drive toward that winning event. Experiential learning provides the insight to the underlying relationships in SCM. Through the use of these tools, the rules of the game are dramatically changed from winning, to mutual benefit.

William Ury, from Harvard University School of Law is one of the leading experts in negotiating to mutual benefit of the parties. Mr. Ury created two landmark works on negotiations, *Getting to Yes* and *Getting Past No.* Collectively these works provide the archetypical roadmap on ethics-based business relationships while still achieving the desired benefit as an outcome of negotiations.

TRANSFORMING FORCES INTO SKILL

The transformation from force-based supply chain management to skill-based SCM is based on two seemingly simple actions: acquiring the skill and tools through education and experience, and the evolution of the professional relationship between the various parts of the supply chain. Education is the simplest aspect of the equation to achieve. The only requirement is the desire to achieve the learning and accessing the resources of coursework, books, and other training resources. Experience is a little more difficult because it requires more than just putting years behind you. Experience is the process of building on and learning from the progression of business encounters. In a simple sense, this means that there needs to be the individual growth of possessing 10 or 20 years of experience, not 1 year of experience 10 or 20 times.

In every aspect of SCM, experience in negotiating is probably the most critical success factor. While the purchasing side of SCM knows of the "trained professional negotiator," many of the other SCM disciplines do not. In fact, in Bill Ury's *Getting Past No*, he describes the reality of what the view is by many in negotiating, which also applies to SCM relationships. "We may all be negotiators, yet many of us don't like to negotiate. We see the negotiations as stressful confrontation. We see ourselves faced with an unpleasant choice. If we are soft in order to preserve the relationship, we end up giving up our position. If we are hard in order to win our position, we strain the relationship or perhaps lose it altogether."[5]

In transforming the force to skill, there are a number of key experience growth factors that affect SCM and relationship management. The first of these is the shift in dealing with the SCM issues. According to Ury, "there is an alternative: joint problem solving. It is neither exclusively soft nor hard, but a combination of each. It is *soft on the people, hard on the problem.* Instead of attacking each other, you attack the problem. In short, you turn face-to-face confrontation into side-by-side problem solving."[6] This approach on issues versus people leads to a second and equally important area of business maturation, that being the truth in the nature of the relationship.

THE COLLABORATIVE RELATIONSHIP[7]

In most industries, SCM professionals describe their approach to supplier relationships as being based on a partnership. Professional and industry journals publish volumes on the approaches that companies take. However, many suppliers would call the relationship anything but a partnership. Nearly any dictionary

5. William Ury, *Getting Past No: Negotiating Your Way from Confrontation to Cooperation*, Revised Edition, (New York, NY., Bantam Doubleday Dell Publishing, 1993), p. 5.
6. William Ury, *Getting Past No*, p. 6.
7. Jeffrey Wincel, "Competitive Supplier Partnerships," *Optimize Magazine*, (August, 2002).

will define partnership as a relationship between two or more parties that share the risks and rewards of a business venture. It may go on to add to the definition that a partnership includes engaging in activities toward a common goal. The only thing in this type of definition that applies to most buy-sell relationships is that the parties are engaged in a business venture. Beyond that, there is limited shared risk and reward, and limited common vision of the ultimate goal. The seller often sees the buyer as forcing all the risk and working to achieve all the reward.

However, there does exist an inextricable relationship between the buyer and seller. In addition, to maximize the benefit to all parties, the relationship has to be one greater than the confrontational "win at any cost" approach that is often found in business. Business relationships in the largest range of the supply chain (i.e., the levels below retail) require successful collaboration to provide for the production, technology, delivery, and competitive cost of a product (or service). Still, these collaborators typically have competing objectives. Balancing the need for collaboration and the competitive objectives can be an effective and cooperative method on which to build a business relationship. This concept is called competitive collaboration.

Competitive collaboration builds on the concepts of Bill Ury described earlier. In addition to separating the people from the issue, it also recognizes the real world factors by which business ventures are motivated. The cooperation has to be based on the answer to the following three questions (from both the customer and seller standpoint):

1. What is the need that must be satisfied (i.e., the part, service, etc.)?
2. How can the potential source satisfy that need?
3. What's in it (i.e., the sourcing solution) for the buyer or the seller?

It's the answer to that third question that drives the nature of the relationship. I believe that competitive collaboration provides the best solution to the need for cooperation.

Competitive collaboration involves both customers and suppliers working together to:

- Consider their own stakeholder needs and present them as the starting point of the buy-sell arrangement. Their competing self-interests thus serve as the basis of the customer-supplier relationship.
- Establish objectives and metrics on which to base success. These metrics (which could include cost/price, design, quality, etc.) become the objective basis on which the value of the relationship is measured.
- Develop product and program for the mutual success of each company.
- Individually measure the objectives and self-interests along the way to validate the ongoing benefit of the relationship
- Base the next agreement, product, or program from the outcomes of the previous competitive collaborative agreement. Both customers and suppliers must objectively evaluate the overall success and value of maintaining the relationship. Customer management and selection is equally important to supplier management and selection.

THE FINAL TRANSFORMATION TO SKILL

The final transformation from force to skill is a construct of the integration of ethics-based business relationships, the use of positive power tools, separation of the issues from the people, and the acknowledgement of the true nature of buy-sell relationships. Lean supply chain management requires these characteristics to be in place to allow for the successful implementation of lean SCM tools.

Lean SCM tools, their use, and the anticipated results are the focus of the next two sections of this book. In setting up for these tools, I want to go back to the work of Bill Ury. Table 3.1 describes the bridges that can take the customer-supplier (or any) negotiation efforts from competitive to cooperative, from people to issues, and from one winner to all winners. Bill's breakthrough strategies are simple but extremely effective, and learning these in detail is worth the read.

Table 3.1 Keys to Negotiation

The Goal: JOINT PROBLEM-SOLVING	BARRIERS TO COOPERATION	Strategy: BREAKTHROUGH NEGOTIATIONS
• People Sitting Side by Side	• Your Reaction • Their Emotion	• Go to the Balcony • Step to Their Side
• Facing the Problem	• Their Emotion	• Reframe
• Reaching a Mutually Satisfactory Agreement	• Their Dissatisfaction • Their Power	• Build Them a Golden Bridge • Use Power to Educate

Adapted from William Ury, *Getting Past No*, p. 13

It is in this mindset that lean SCM is based. Breakthrough lean SCM strategies capable of delivering dramatic and sustained improvement are both at once simple and complex. They are simple in the structure and use of the tools, but complex (not difficult) in the way in which these tools are used for a comprehensive supply chain strategy.

CASE STUDY 3.2

Questions

1. How should DSW respond to its customer with respect to the sourcing proposal considering that the current part was sourcing with 18 percent gross profit and 3.5 percent pretax, and was two years into a four-year contract with 4 percent annual price reductions; and that the new part was quoted at 17 percent and 3 percent profits rates and 3.5 percent annual price reductions.
2. To meet the annual customer price reductions, what can DSW do to reduce its cost structure?
3. What does DSW's customer's purchasing organization believe about its ability to negotiate the new product sourcing and potentially achieve incremental reduction on existing business?

Answers

1. DSW agreed to the incremental reduction on the existing business, believing that it had no choice if it wanted to secure the future sourcing. DSW's plans for this incremental reduction would include reductions in overhead and prime costs in attempt to drive gross and pretax margins to acceptable levels.
2. To meet the annual customer price reductions DSW accelerated a re-engineering effort in reducing its overhead cost structure (read here "downsizing"). These efforts would directly affect the program support the customer would receive.

3. The customer's purchasing organization expressed no reservations about the tactics it employed for this sourcing activity. In fact, when questioned regarding the approach they used, they responded with the statement that this was the changing nature of business relationships and to continue to be a "preferred" supplier meant complying with the approach.

SECTION II

The Crisis Environment

4

Defining the Crisis Environment

Defining a crisis environment in procurement and SCM can be a difficult proposition. It's difficult because our profession often seems to be in crisis for a number of different reasons. Simply said, in many industries, times may always be difficult or in crisis, and the difficulty always continues.

Crisis can be caused because of the lack of availability of critically needed production components, such as the semiconductor shortages in 1998 and 1999. Crisis can be caused because of a loss in market and industry confidence exemplified by the technology and communications slowdowns in 2001 and 2002. Bad corporate investments or bad corporate management can also cause crisis.

In examining the SCM tools available for managing these crises, the cause of the crisis will make little difference. What will be of importance is recognizing the need for a unique set of tools through which to navigate the crisis environment.

TYPICAL CRISIS CONDITIONS

Effective SCM becomes more important when the crisis that a company is trying to weather is a financial one. It will be this

CASE STUDY 4.1

To offset the decline in the net pretax profits of the company, DSW, at the urging of its main customers, began to expand its business holdings in foreign markets. Through a combination of greenfield expansion and company acquisition, the product line, manufacturing capacity, and customers served were greatly expanded for DSW. DSW believed that its customers would commit substantial business growth opportunity because of the new global presence—having followed the customers to their new markets.

Although the organic and acquisition growth strategies were based upon strict business plan payback evaluations, with its expanded international presence DSW found itself in serious financial trouble. Two concurrent issues brought about this crisis. The first was that the due diligence evaluation DSW conducted on its acquired businesses was overly optimistic with respect to debt load, product profitability, and opportunity for expansion in the acquired markets. The second issue was a general industry and economic slowdown resulting in a stagnation of business growth opportunities and a decline in current product demand.

Questions:

1. What other business realities might have contributed to DSW's financial problems, challenging their ability to solve them?
2. How would you anticipate DSW focused its efforts on resolving these business issues?
3. What would be the supply chain response or involvement in managing the financial crisis at DSW?

assumption of financial crisis on which the SCM tools will be built. Defining a crisis environment is pretty straightforward. Economically, these difficult times are characterized by slow or no revenue growth. The cause of the zero growth can be driven by either general economic slowdown affecting all competitors in a particular market or segment, or is brought about due to poor corporate management.

Generally, the financial impact of the slow or zero revenue growth is that the organization's overhead and SG&A costs have not slowed in parity with the revenue slowdown. This imbalance effectively reduces the gross profit absorption of the overhead costs. In contracting markets, this impact is amplified to an even greater extent. New business opportunities by which to offset these impacts are greatly limited. It is often due to these environmental and situational conditions that SCM organizations are faced with increased material and transportation cost requests. The ability to offset the requests through business leverage opportunities is limited.

THE BAD NEWS OF CRISIS

Two universal features affect SCM in crisis. As previously mentioned, the first of these is that the revenue growth conditions do not allow an organization to sell its way back to profitability, or to leverage-buy its way to profitability. Most companies attempt to use a sell approach to increase gross profit and pretax margins by better allocating expenses over a larger base. The buy side of this solution gains focus when the other methods fail to work. However, without the volumes, many SCM professionals seem not to understand the direction they need to head to achieve the needed savings.

SCM employees often take on an increased importance in an organization where sales and profits are being squeezed or are declining. This second universal effect of crisis often comes out of desperation from executive management when nothing else seems to work. There comes an increased and immediate pressure on the supply chain organization to achieve savings through whatever means possible. The need to achieve immediate and substantial savings often overtakes the longer-term need of remaining focused on fundamental business practices and on future as well as immediate needs. The ability to retain a strategic focus is compromised.

When the crisis is being driven from industry or segment slowdowns, two additional truths exist. The first of these is that as your competitors face and react to the same factors driving you, they typically are aggressively eyeing your business to achieve their own sales growth. It is here that the character of a company's ability to implement successful strategies to weather the storm is tested. If the competition remains calm, implements effective slow-down strategies, and focuses efforts for both the long and short term, it is they who will undoubtedly grow despite the adversity. If the opposite is true, then the competition will need to react to your efforts.

Unfortunately, just as you are affected by the economic factors of a slowing economy or segment, so to are your customers. Whereas the pursuit of cost and price reductions has regularly occurred from your customers, it is now likely to be accelerated. The ability to reduce your cost base is lessened by the loss of growth opportunity, so reducing overhead and SG&A costs becomes even more important. Also, with a lessened ability to achieve price reductions via cost savings, resourcing-based cost savings gain more importance.

NOT ALL NEWS IS BAD

The key to any business challenge is not to panic and to find the uncommon and creative solutions to the most challenging problems. With every set of bad news items, there always exists the good news. That holds true in a business crisis. The first piece of good news in a crisis borne of an industry or segment slowdown is that you are not in this alone. Your competitors are faced with the same challenge, trying to avoid the same profit and pricing squeeze. Being the most prepared for these events by having established system approaches capable of reacting to varying business conditions can help you outlast the competition.

Although a company does not have the ability to increase leverage through increases in sales or purchases, the existing business that is procured (whether product, service, or transportation) becomes far more important to the incumbent suppliers. The leverage opportunities exist not in the ability to gain significant new pieces of business, but in the opportunity to keep existing business. Just as the bad news is that your competitors are chasing your business, the good news is that your suppliers are chasing each other's business.

Economic and industry slowdowns need be viewed as a market shift, with the appropriate market-based tools used to capture these shifts. Where capacity becomes more readily available and drives down the price, the acquisition strategy has to adapt in recognition of these movements. The approaches taken here can be either confrontational with a "whipsaw"-like effect, or collaborative using supplier resources as inputs to capture the efficiency.

Crisis challenges can be seen as a positive basis for change, not a negative condition in which traditional approaches fail to work. Although all the major industries' SCM professionals want to view themselves as enlightened and creative, the truth lies more in the tried and true strategies. The tried and true, however, typically fail in the most challenging environments and the fallback usually becomes ultimatums and a general negative spiral into confrontation.

So the good news is that since the easy gains are gone and the simple approaches no longer work, the SCM group can develop and explore new and creative ways of meeting the companies' demands and improvement requirements. The tools described in the following chapters represent some of those creative ways.

Finally, because the situation can be so critical, any improvement beyond the existing plan is viewed as good news. This reality provides for the necessary positive reinforcement of even the smallest of steps. By using the opportunity for change, and reinforcing the moves by acknowledging the contribution, the SCM organization can institutionalize these new approaches as the strategic basis for its daily activities.

KEEPING STRATEGIC

A fundamental part of human nature seems to be to fall back on the easiest activities when faced with a challenge. That is, those actions that are the simplest to define, the simplest to implement, and the simplest to measure are usually the ones we apply to a business in crisis. These efforts usually include staffing reductions, supplier consolidation, elimination of longer-term strategic initiatives, and an intense, but limited, focus on the immediate short-term demands.

Because most organizations accept these short-term problem resolution efforts, there is often a loss of sight of the strategic efforts. This reality results in companies going from one short-term crisis to another, never preparing the business processes capable of dealing with the issues automatically. With each new challenge comes a new set of limited approaches to deal with the challenge. What was done last time may or may not be done this time, and what needs to be done in the future never happens. This entire approach is typified by the annual business plan activity of most U.S. companies. Last year's efforts, which have never really been pursued, are tossed out for a new set of initiatives that become the new marching orders.

With all this in mind, is it likely or even possible that an organization has the ability to keep a strategic focus in a time of crisis? The answer is simply yes. The ability to do so requires a shift in thinking from short term to short-term *strategic*.

SHORT-TERM STRATEGIC

The idea of strategy in the short term is probably foreign to most businesses. While strategic tools or initiatives might be used, the concept of strategy is usually thought of in terms of actions and objectives to be taken in the distant future, having very little to do with the present. Short-term strategic makes use of some of the common short-term tools, and incorporates them into multiphased SCM (or other business) strategies. Ultimately the efforts are designed to provide the needed short-term improvements while maintaining the business systems and focus on the longer term.

Lean manufacturing and lean supply chain techniques are based on the idea of change—specifically, change in the sense of continued improvement and efficiency efforts incorporated into the daily operating practice of a company. Two types of change affect the timing and focus of the lean initiatives pursued by an organization: kaizen (traditional change) and kaikaku (radical change). These change elements lend themselves to the needs of long- and short-term strategic efforts. It is the selection of the appropriate change methodology that enables a company to remain committed to broader business needs and strategies, while dealing with the reality of the short-term crisis.

CHANGES BIG AND SMALL

Anyone who has been faced with an organizational crisis has probably personally experienced or witnessed some sort of hero syndrome. The hero syndrome is the idea that with one heroic act, one major effort, or just one home run an individual or team can solve the problems of the company. For example, the hope is often that everything will be fine if the sales group gets the one new big contract or negotiates the big price increases. Administratively, as mentioned before, the approach might be to take care of everything with one large staffing or overhead cost reduction. And in SCM, this is seen by the big cost and price reduction activity. These so-called heroic efforts themselves don't necessarily pose the problem. The problem lies in the fact that in difficult times the tendency is only to swing for the fences.

These efforts represent the radical short-term efforts most organizations use in dealing with crisis. Large or radical changes are not necessarily a bad thing. In fact, when used appropriately, these change efforts can provide for a fresh way of thinking and a creative avenue to better change. When these techniques are used exclusively to resolve crisis, they can inhibit stability and may foster confusion as to the path to the future.

Along with the radical change, there needs to be a tempering balance of traditional change and improvement techniques. By balancing these efforts, both short- and long-term SCM improvement and savings strategies can occur. The change theories of kaizen and kaikaku can keep balance in pursuing the needed changes and improvements.

KAIZEN AND KAIKAKU

An underlying methodology and philosophy should bind the change concepts we've been talking about in their implementation and execution. Change for change's sake is not normally viewed as a worthwhile pursuit. Change for a purpose, and change with structure and intent are normally viewed as the most effective. However, all change will have its naysayers. By utilizing

Figure 4.1 Kaizen

structured approaches to change, the naysayers will have less audience in their complaints and resistance.

Anyone who has been around North American manufacturing during the past 10 years has probably heard this word. Kaizen (reprensented by Figure 4.1) is part of the Japanese manufacturing philosophy that simply means making continuous improvements (usually small increments) in quality, cost, productivity, delivery, etc. Most purchasing improvement plans are based on using some variations of kaizen to achieve improvements in performance, cost savings, and so on. It is likely however, that many, if not most SCM practitioners are unaware of the kaizen philosophies by which they are planning for and implementing their strategy.[1] Kaizen is generally the preferred method of identifying opportunities for change and implementing them in a controlled manner. Literally, kaizen means change for the better. In Yasuhiro Monden's book, he describes kaizen as the method to reduce organizational slack through the "continuous implementation of smaller improvement activities."[2]

Crisis, on the other hand, is characterized by a critical need to make rapid and marked improvements. However, even these changes can occur in a managed environment. In fact, manag-

1. Jeffrey Wincel, "A Practitioners View of Strategic Procurement," SCMR.
2 Yasuhiro Moden, *Toyota Production System—An Integrated Approach to Just-in-Time,* Engineering & Management Press, 3rd Edition, 1998, pp. 199.

Figure 4.2 Kaikaku

ing large or radical change requires an even more structured and focused approach to ensure success and sustainability.

Although commonly used in many manufacturing environments, TPS practitioners may not use kaikaku, or perhaps not be aware of the term, preferring to remain with traditional change efforts. This is certainly true of most supply chain professionals. Kaikaku (represented by Figure 4.2) is also a description of change, but it refers to radical or dramatic change. The reason the lean practitioners may not be aware of the term is that radical change is not necessary in an environment where incremental improvement has been a way of life, and success is engrained in the nature of business. Kaikaku really only becomes necessary when the hole you are in is too deep to dig out of. Literally, the term means reformation, renovation, or reorganization. The TPS master may know this concept as radi-

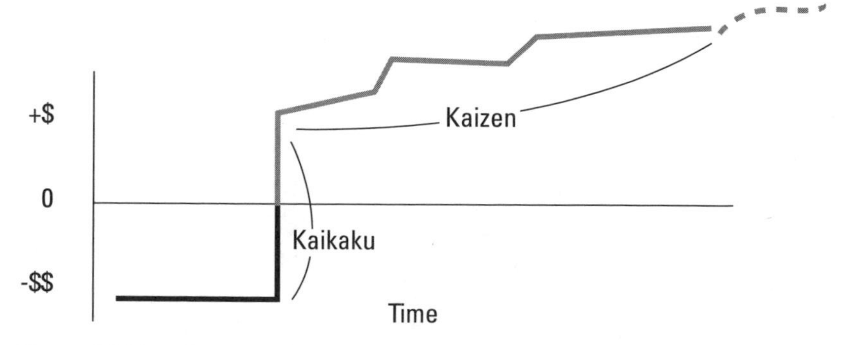

Figure 4.3 From Radical to Incremental Change

cal kaizen or a similar term. Perhaps in a business sense the easiest understanding of when and why kaikaku is needed can be demonstrated in Figure 4.3.

When the situation demands radical action, kaikaku is a planned method designed to achieve the critical business improvements. In many cases the improvements are needed to save the business. Planned well, kaikaku activities can move the business to where the more traditional kaizen methods can be employed. The structuring of a turn-around plan based on kaikaku and kaizen concepts provides a structured approach during a time when there is a tendency to throw caution to the wind.

CASE STUDY 4.2

Questions

1. What other business realities might have contributed to DSW's financial problems, challenging their ability to solve them?
2. How would you anticipate DSW focused its efforts on resolving these business issues?
3. What would be the supply chain response or involvement in managing the financial crisis at DSW?

Answers

1. Other business realities at DSW included a very traditional view on company value directly related to stock price. Although a clear earnings to price relationship was difficult to establish, a pursuit of immediate cost reductions was determined necessary to raise stock price. The organization was not structured in either organization or business approach to react to the needed reductions while maintaining a growth and improvement strategy. Also, the belief that customers would reward the expansion into the new markets was not backed by any customer commitment and did not provide the revenue to support the infrastructure that was put into place to support the move.
2. DWS's initial reaction to the crisis was largely what might be expected. There was pricing shot across the bow with the customers, requesting (or even demanding) price increases that were not granted. The ability to get the increases was severely limited by the lack of DSW to be

able to implement any action in the event that the increases were not granted.

Organizationally, DWS planned for and implemented a staffing reduction plan that largely proved to be ineffective. While the savings in operating costs appeared to have had a positive effect on the income statement, the severance costs associated with the downsizing significantly reduced the available capital for other investment needs. In addition, much of the work required at DSW could no longer be accomplished, and within 12 months a significant number of the eliminated positions were refilled.

Initially the executive team had pushed the SCM organization down the traditional road of demands, threats, and unilateral price reductions with its suppliers, without any consideration for the backdrop by which these price reductions would need to occur. The SCM organization was able to resist this initial effort and develop and deploy a crisis plan.

3. After resisting the initial executive management push to the tried and true but failed cost and price improvement practices, the SCM organization was able to develop and implement a multiphased cost improvement plan utilizing kaizen and kaikaku SCM concepts. The resulting improvements provided a net 5 percent improvement in cost within the first 12 to 18 months, achieving record savings levels. This was accomplished in a collaborative way with new and existing suppliers, and provided for improvements in quality and delivery in addition to cost.

5

Crisis Plan Background and Phase 1: Acquisition Team Formation

THE GROUNDWORK[1]

A simple fact of strategic plans is also an unfortunate fact—that is, most strategic plans die on the drawing board because they lack an implementation profile to deliver the plan and results. Before detailing the crisis plan it is more important to describe how to develop an implementation strategy. The ideas are simple but critical to success. The organizations described, such as supplier development, may have different names (or may not exist at all) in individual companies, but the disciplines they represent require critical thought processes. The following sections outline the steps to make a purchasing/SCM plan work:

PREPARATION

The buyer and supplier development representatives meet to discuss each supplier's individual situation. This team reviews the supplier's commodity, the supplier's history for cost reductions,

1. Acknowledgement needs to be given to Mr. Steve Alsbro in the initial development of the basis of the plan strategy. Mr. Alsbro was a colleague at TRW Inc., and is currently director of global commodity development for Whirlpool Corp.

long-term agreements, and current cost reduction position. It is equally important to gauge the supplier's attitude and business relationship with you as a customer. If the plan is to be a success, an open and honest relationship must exist within the workforce and team members. The team identifies the types of opportunities at each supplier, and which of the cost improvement tools would work best.

MANAGEMENT REVIEW

The supplier is invited to participate in a management review meeting. This meeting is scheduled for about one hour at the buyer's location. A senior management team is expected to represent the supplier. The agenda should include:

1. The program concept.
2. The value expected to be derived for both you and the supplier.
3. The steps, or procedure that will be followed.
4. The program guidelines.
5. The shared cost reduction strategy.

During the course of the meeting buyers and suppliers should discuss:

1. Timing and scheduling.
2. Identification of a supplier champion.
3. Any potential implementation costs incurred by the suppliers.
4. How those costs will be handled.
5. The supplier's commitment at all levels.

The supplier will be expected to come prepared to discuss these issues. The goal of the meeting is to establish a clear and mutually agreeable approach to reduce costs for both parties.

IMPLEMENTATION

Each of the tools used in the crisis plan will have a different implementation profile. This will be discussed in detail for each tool. During this step the supplier may be requested to perform tasks that must be completed in a timely fashion. Once the commitment has been made at the management review it is expected that a program will move forward without delay. Because this section deals with single events, or campaign style programs, it is critical that both you and the supplier meet the program timing as it is defined.

CLOSURE

Once the project is completed, and the changes made and proven, the buyer will be responsible for authorizing the price reduction. The buyer does this in writing to the supplier. The buyer will issue a part change notice or purchase order amendment and the price change will be in effect.

These items represent a brief outline of how to handle and manage the overall crisis program. While it may seem elementary, experience has demonstrated that without detailing the steps of implementation, the results are greatly jeopardized and credibility can be lost both internally and externally (with suppliers). Of equal importance to the success of the plan is clearly defining what needs to be done, what steps and processes are going to be used, and what the expected outcomes are. If these elements are not clearly understood by the internal team or by the supplier, the process needs to immediately stop. Expediency in finishing the plan in spite of a lack of clarity is not something that can be overlooked.

CASE STUDY 5.1

The international SCM organization at DSW had only limited success in integrating its worldwide operations, and using its global influence. The development and implementation of its crisis plan would require the integration of its various global activities. While the development and implementation of the SCM plan would require significant resources in personnel, there remained the need to run the day-to-day business operations. New product sourcing and program launch activities continued to occur, along with the need to meet customer demands on current production parts.

Questions

1. How could DSW's supply chain organization effectively coordinate its global activities, and what roadblocks might they encounter?
2. What methods or mechanisms could DSW put into place to balance the needs of the plan implementation with the daily requirements?
3. Who were the key players or organizations in the DSW work?

THE CRISIS PLAN ELEMENTS

The individual crisis plan elements can be grouped into five phases. Phases I through III can be equated with kaikaku approaches. These include:

I. Acquisition team formation.
II. Price benchmarking.
III. Short-term process improvement (SPI).

They tend to be largely sequential and are critically time dependant.

Phases IV and V are the kaizen steps:

IV. Value analysis/value engineering (VA/VE).

V. Lean manufacturing.

Phase IV begins concurrent with the final steps of Phase III. It is in this overlap where the kaikaku-kaizen transition really takes hold. Phase V is the implementation of TPS-like production systems at the supplier, or the introduction of flow kaizen within the entire operation. Figure 5.1 shows the relationship between the crisis plan action and the change strategy associated with the action.

Savings Techniques

Big changes—Kaikaku

- Price benchmarking
- Short term process improvements (SPI) or "point kaizen"

改革

Small changes—Kaizen

- Value analysis / value engineering
- Lean manufacturing (TPS) or "flow kaizen"

Figure 5.1

Once you begin to enter phases IV and V, a more traditional approach to procurement strategies can be taken. In both the kaizen and kaikaku actions, the need to follow through on the plan elements is critical to optimal success. It is easy to lose opportunities as time is extended. Leverage opportunities are created through the implementation of the plan elements, but they can be quickly and easily lost if not capitalized on immediately. Figure 5.2 provides the timing elements of each of the plan steps and reflects the serial or parallel nature of the change activities.

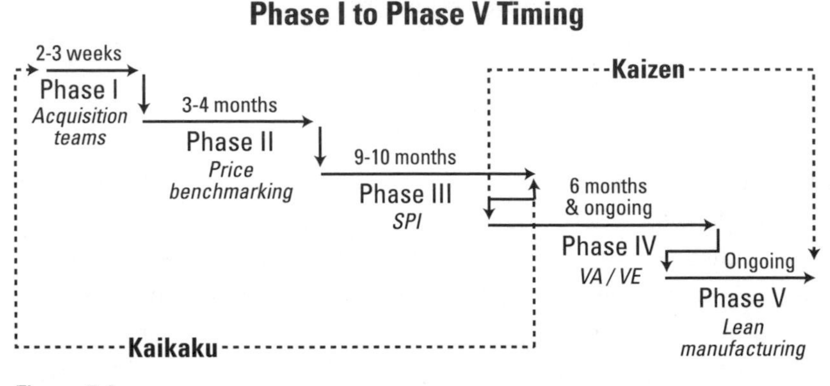

Figure 5.2

COST IS THE BOTTOM LINE

The very nature of the crisis itself requires that the SCM plan deliver significant and immediate cost savings. The linking of short- and long-term efforts through kaizen and kaikaku provides for different cost improvement features. Organizations that have some level of strategic supplier and commodity development activity usually experience an associated cost improvement curve with these efforts. In a time of crisis, the level (i.e., the amount) of cost improvement, the timing of cost improvement, and the sustainability of cost improvement become critical issues.

A typical tier-one company can generally expect a savings profile of 1 percent to 3 percent annual price improvement from its supply base. The maximum savings level is achieved in approximately year 3, with declining savings in years 4 and 5.[2] The incorporation of kaikaku actions pulls ahead a portion of the savings potential into years 0 and 1, and provides a contribution for increasing the maximum savings potential. The kaizen

2. The savings profile described here and in Figure 5.3 are derived from observed savings patterns for automotive tier-one suppliers from the period of 1993–2002.

actions provide the balance on the increase to maximum savings potential and extend the sustainability beyond the three-

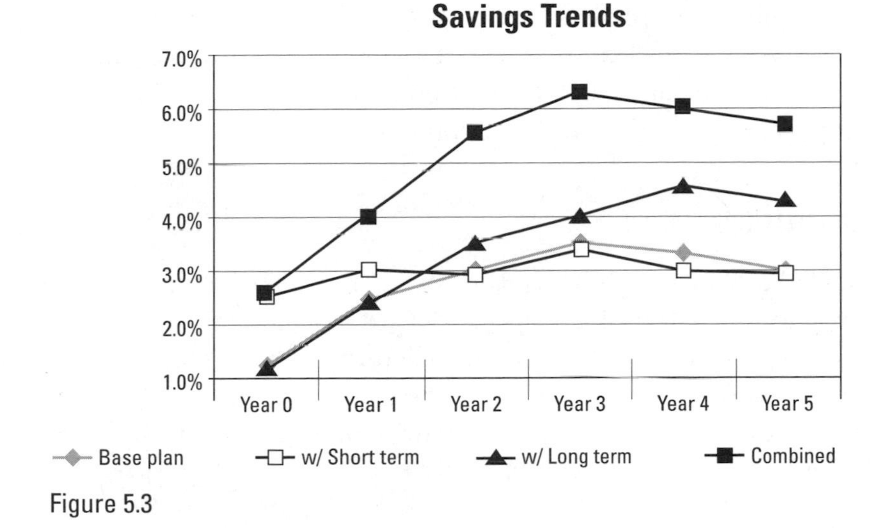

Figure 5.3

year average. Figure 5.3 demonstrates the traditional savings curve when supplemented with kaikaku savings only; supplemented with kaizen savings only, and finally supplemented with both kaizen and kaikaku savings for maximum benefit.

The traditional savings profile is typically based on achieving market-based savings only. These saving are achieved by resourcing actions, consolidation efforts, and perhaps even by multiyear price improvement contracts. The crisis plan includes market mechanisms, but also addresses process, design, and system costs in developing price reduction ideas.

PHASE I: ACQUISITION TEAM FORMATION

In the beginning of this chapter, I discussed the importance of having an implementation plan to achieve the maximum benefits of the crisis strategy. The rest of this chapter focuses on phase I of the crisis plan, acquisition team formation, including a description and the procedure by which it occurs. Chapters 6, 7, 8, and 9 examine the remaining phases of an SCM crisis plan. The goal of these chapters is to provide information that will help SCM professionals ensure the clarity of the strategy, provide a clear roadmap by which the process can be implemented, and explain the verification process, which provides closure to the savings identified.

DEFINITION

Kaikaku teams is a concept borrowed from lean manufacturing practices where problem specialists are assigned to assume control of and attack significant manufacturing issues. While seldom used, these teams represent a crisis management team where daily operating control of all or part of an organization is turned over to specialists. These specialists have the single responsibility to identify and correct the issues causing the crisis. Typically using radical change methods, these teams maintain responsibility until the changes are well underway, and then transition back to the operating team.

The purchasing application of kaikaku teams is called acquisition teams. The purpose in defining these teams as acquisition teams is to ensure the full consideration of all acquisition-related issues, not simply price. Among these issues are quality and manufacturing capability features, design capability, location and logistics, and others. These teams assume the control and management of critical commodities to achieve significant cost improvement, quality improvement, and supply base consolidation.

IMPLEMENTATION PROCEDURE

The acquisition team fully assumes the daily commodity planning and sourcing responsibilities from the local purchasing team and constructs a compressed improvement plan. The daily purchasing responsibilities and part availability remains with the local team. The team includes a procurement or commodity planning specialist and a supplier development or quality engineer as permanent team members. The procurement team member serves as the team leader and remains independent of previous commodity and supplier development history. The need for this independence is to ensure a fresh approach that isn't subject to the historic baggage that the commodity or individual suppliers may present. The change process and acquisition process need to be the primary driver of the action, not anecdotal or subjective decisions.

As needed, team members may include product engineering, tooling engineering, program management and customer support, manufacturing, and the existing commodity buyer. This team conducts the individual supplier and commodity analysis and plan development discussed previously. Weekly local reviews and monthly management reviews verify the implementation action and pace of the activities defined by the acquisition team. The team has full authority for all commodity pricing, sourcing, and consolidation activities as approved by the purchasing or supply chain executive. Once the plan is significantly in place, implementation responsibility is returned to the local purchasing group.

CASE STUDY 5.2

Questions

1. How could DSW's supply chain organization effectively coordinate its global activities, and what roadblocks might they encounter?
2. What methods or mechanisms could DSW put into place to balance the needs of the plan implementation with the daily requirements?
3. Who were the key players or organizations in the DSW work?

Answers

1. DSW broadened its implementation of a "matrix" organization whereby the planning process and sourcing strategies were centralized within a global structure. The regional implementation provided matrix reporting to the local operating management to ensure that the daily requirements of customer support were addressed. Additionally, the global resources were used to staff the acquisition teams without the need for adding or redeploying staff. Through the development of strategic and transactions sections of the organization, DSW's ability to service the needs of the global organization was enhanced.
2. The structure of the acquisition team allowed DSW to maintain its daily responsibilities while freeing up resources to focus on the crisis management. Initially this proved to be a challenge for DSW. Executive management, while wanting the focus to be on resolving the company's financial crisis, had difficulty appreciating the value of having multiple teams responsible for various aspects of the same company.

3. Perhaps the most difficult issue to accept was that the current commodity buyer or program buyer was no longer responsible for the critical sourcing decisions, but for a time relegated to an entirely transactional role. However, the buyer remained a key player in that the final delivery of the plan elements would fall back to this buyer. Other major players included supplier development, quality, manufacturing, and customer/program management.

6

Phase II: Price Benchmarking

How often has a supply chain organization had its strategic plan put on hold because of the need of the company's economy, with one priority in mind—the money? Chapter 5 described the economic factors that create a business crisis. In this crisis it's necessary to quickly deliver improvements to the bottom line. But how is this done without giving up the future?

When immediate savings are needed, the procurement side of supply chain management often gets lazy. The typical practice is what I call "dialing for dollars." The purchasing executive fires off a letter to all the suppliers demanding a price reduction with either the subtle or not so subtle threat of loss of business. The buyers and managers then follow up with the calls to the account managers and sales VPs pursuing the savings. In some industries, the suppliers may not even have a choice. In 2001 a major automotive OEM not only demanded an across-the-board 5 percent price reduction, but implemented it unilaterally with an automatic purchase order price reduction. Only through supplier threats of supply interruption (by those suppliers big enough to make the threats) were some of the reductions lessened or reversed.

CASE STUDY 6.1

DSW's corporate organization was structured to support business in two major industry groups. Both of the product groups were extremely sensitive to market fluctuations, and while these fluctuations were cyclical in nature, the timing of the cycles could not accurately be predicted. In addition, segment 1 had delivered the majority of the profits for the company allowing investment and growth into the unrelated segment 2. However, the segment 1 prices and profits were deteriorating quickly, jeopardizing DSW's ability to gain market leadership into segment 2 just as it was in an upward swing in its business cycle.

To improve the overall profitability, all the segment 1 businesses were given significant immediate cost reduction targets. Within the supply chain activity, this included supplier pricing reductions and total cost of acquisition reductions (e.g., quality improvements, freight reductions).

DSW's supply chain organization already had a strategic plan in place in which total supplier capabilities (including price competitiveness) were being reviewed and were to be the determinants of the "permanent" supply base. However, the implementation of the plan was over a three-year period, and this timing did not support the immediate financial needs. Therefore, the strategic plan was put on hold.

Questions

1. In pursuing the immediate cost savings, what steps did DSW initially take with its suppliers—that is, what alternatives did they have to choose from?
2. What could the anticipated level of success be with each of the possibilities identified in question 1?
3. What steps would the DSW supply chain executive need to take with respect to maintaining a future focus?

PHASE II—PRICE BENCHMARKING

Somewhere in the development of supply chain management, assessing the market became a "bastardized" approach where any company with a pulse was considered to be a viable source, and any price from those suppliers was considered legitimate. It was unlikely that this "alley shop" approach was going to yield new suppliers, but the prices they reported were used to "whipsaw" the prices from the existing suppliers. This approach served to make any evaluation of market shifts seem sinister.

Price benchmarking is a structured method to evaluate shifts that have occurred in the marketplace since the initial sourcing of the product. Factors such as market demand and associated available capacity, introduction of new or advanced manufacturing technology, additional entrants to the market, and other commercial considerations affect the "correct" current market price.

Definition

Purchase price benchmarking is the practice whereby market analysis, cost estimating tools, affordable cost targeting, and design/manufacturing analysis are used to establish the fair market drive price.

Implementation Procedure

To quantify the near-term price reduction potential, the acquisition team establishes a component-level price benchmark for current production items. A price benchmark is a composite value of affordable cost targets (prices to which you can afford to purchase the part to achieve internal profitability targets), design- and manufacturing-based cost estimates (the cost plus estimate of prices), and market-driven factors such as inflations, commodity market prices movements, and currency fluctuations. The weighting of each of these factors is subjectively determined by the acquisition team and applied to the final price target.

ASPECTS OF THE PHASE II PROCESS

1) The identification of manufacturing difficulty and complexity stratification; 2) an assessment of source change potential—i.e., the feasibility of source changes based on conditions such as proprietary rights, customer directives, complexity of tooling, etc.; 3) the development of affordable cost targets; and 4) competitive market test results. Incumbent suppliers will be included in the market test with opportunity to retain business at target price. Where supply relationships warrant, the incumbent supplier will be given a last right of refusal to the market price.

Upon the availability of the price benchmark data, price negotiations to the benchmark level occur. The prevailing benchmark price plus amortization of tooling and source change costs establishes the maximum price payment level for any component. Incumbent suppliers unable to achieve the benchmark pricing levels are phased out.

The acquisition team remains responsible for any resulting resourcing activity, including, but not limited to: material bank calculations and development; tooling refurbishment plans; exit PPAP (production part approval process) and CMM (coordinate measuring machine) layout; drawing revision to manufactured accepted part designs; on-site tooling transfer, both pick-up and delivery; process set-up and approval; initial part trials and tuning; level V PPAP;[1] and first shipment for production.

BUILDING AN AFFORDABLE COST TARGET (ACT)

The development of an affordable cost target seems to be a fundamentally simple task, however, most procurement organiza-

---

1. Level V PPAP refers to an automotive industry standard for production part approval process based on the standards established by the Automotive Industries Action Group (AIAG). PPAP level submissions are determined individually by customer requirements and may vary depending on action taken requiring approval.

tions seem at a loss to adequately structure an approach. Most use a cost estimate in place of an ACT, essentially following a "cost plus" process. In this practice, the value of material, labor, machine time, etc. are estimated; an "appropriate" mark-up applied; and a price derived. The fallacy with this process is that it assumes the estimated values from the suppliers' processes and business practices have any relation to best-in-class cost structures. Also, this process fails to take in customer perceived value of the product (or service) being provided. Overengineering or overprocessing results in a higher cost, but if the customer does not perceive the value and is unwilling to pay for the premium, the cost estimate is meaningless.

The following cost setting process represents only one of many approaches that could be used to arrive at a similar end. This cost setting approach uses the value content of a costed bill of material (BOM) as a percentage of the cost of goods, and links it to gross margin rates. The following example will demonstrate how to derive an ACT on an existing base of parts. The process can be just as easily applied to a new part using a surrogate comparison.

Existing Part:	
Current Sales Price	$115
Total Cost of Goods Sold	$100
Total Costed BOM	$ 55 (55% of COGS)
Current Gross Margin (115-100)/115	13%
Target Gross Margin	25%

BOM Components	**Price**	**% of BOM**	**% of COGS**
Component #1	$25	45.5%	25%
Component #2	$12	21.8%	12%
Component #3	$10	18.2%	10%
Component #4	$ 8	14.5%	8%

To achieve a target margin of 25 percent with fixed sales price of \$115, total COGS must = x:

(\$115 – x)/\$115 = .25

\$115 – x = .25 * \$115

\$115 – x = \$28.75

\$115 – \$28.75 = x

\$86.25 = x

Based on this calculation the total COGS cannot exceed \$86.25 to reach the target gross margin of 25 percent.

Two methods of calculation can now determine the costed BOM total.

1. From the initial calculation, material content is 55% of COGS or \$47.44 of the new COGS total (55% × 86.25 = \$47.44 — a reduction of \$7.56).
2. From the calculation there needs to be a reduction in COGS from \$100 to \$86.25 or a \$13.75 reduction. At 55% content, \$7.56 needs to be reduced from the material cost (55% × \$13.75).

To calculate the new target component prices, either the percent of new COGS or BOM Cost can be used. The following numbers show both methods maintaining the BOM and COGS relationship from above.

BOM Components	**New Price**	**% of BOM**	**% of COGS**
Component #1	\$21.56	45.5%	25%
BOM Based	\$47.44	45.5%	
COGS Based	\$86.25	25%	
Component #2	\$10.35	21.8%	12%
Component #3	\$ 8.63	18.2%	10%
Component #4	\$ 6.90	14.5%	8%

The method just presented makes a number of obvious assumptions. Among these is the assumption that the shortfall to gross margin is equally shared by material and other factors in a COGS calculation. This becomes a significant factor when determining a price benchmark target. If in initial sourcing an ACT setting process was used and achieved, the repeating of this process may be unfairly be targeting supplier content for profit attainment. Operational variances in labor and overhead may be the primary factor in missing gross margin targets.

However, even if purchase cost targets were initially met, it is possible that the market driven sales price for your product has declined without similar adjustments in the component prices. In this case, the reestablishment of affordable cost targets reflects actual changes and is appropriate. The flow-through of market demands reflects customer expectations and needs to be evident in all aspects of the supply chain.

The development and use of affordable cost targets should become an integral part of supply chain management and all sourcing activities. Figure 6.1 demonstrates how an ACT process can become an imbedded piece of a total market-based pricing methodology. The use of targets and design for assembly and design for manufacturing (DFA/DFM) models enables a company to provide a product that satisfies customer demands at profit rates which meet or exceed internal requirements.

MEASURING THE MARKET MOVEMENT

The second primary factor in the development of price benchmark targets is the evaluation of market conditions. Here, too, exist various methodologies, including monitoring producer price inflation (PPI) or deflation rates;[2] utilizing standard

2. Specific commodity level historic PPI rates can be located at *www.bls.gov* for material price movement in the U.S.. These indexes allow for information at a summary level, or at a specific configuration detail.

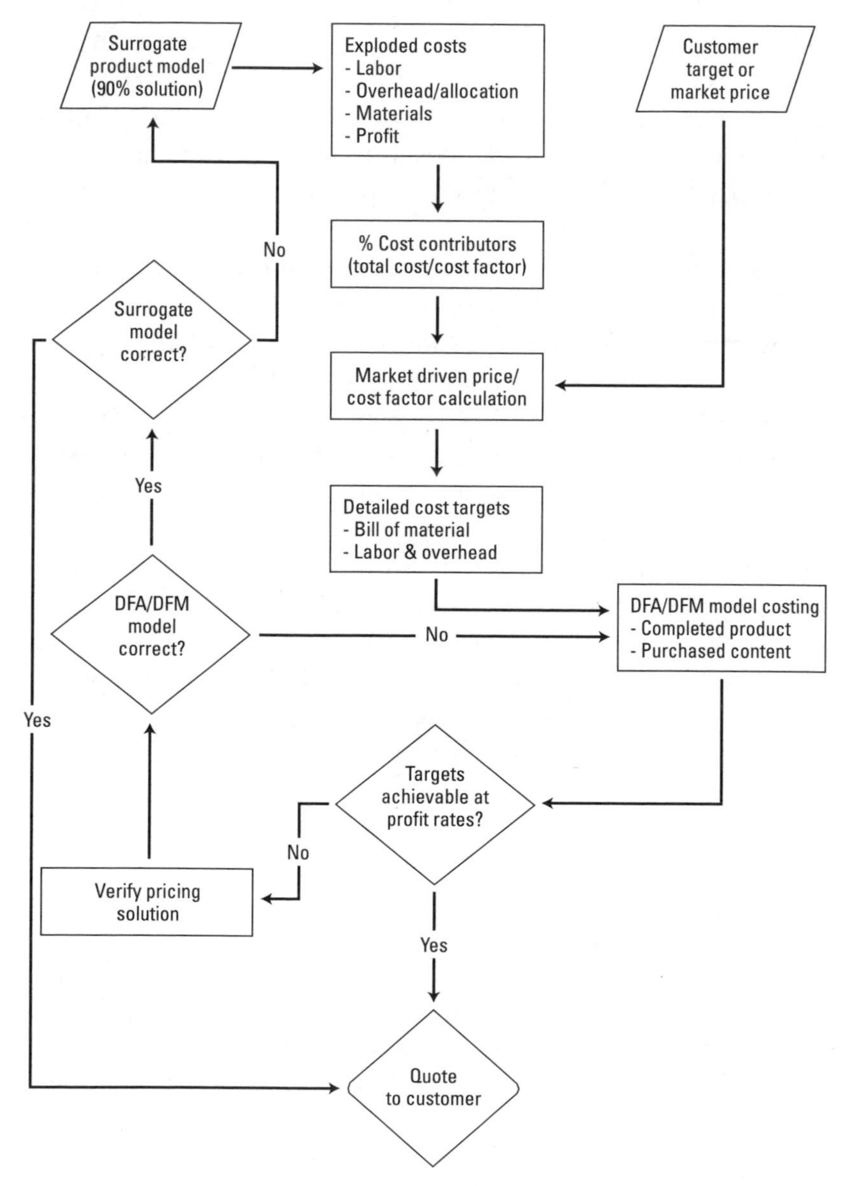
Production Quotation Model
Product development input
Customer unit input
Surrogate product model (90% solution)
Exploded costs
- Labor
- Overhead/allocation
- Materials
- Profit
Customer target or market price
% Cost contributors (total cost/cost factor)
No
Surrogate model correct?
Market driven price/ cost factor calculation
Yes
Detailed cost targets
- Bill of material
- Labor & overhead
DFA/DFM model correct?
No
DFA/DFM model costing
- Completed product
- Purchased content
Yes
Targets achievable at profit rates?
No
Verify pricing solution
Yes
Quote to customer

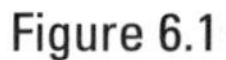
Figure 6.1

indexes to gage potential price movements, such as metals, plastics, etc; and gathering supply and supplier intelligence from industry and professional publications. All of these sources and methods are valid. What they are limited to, however, is often a macro view of market. Often, a missing piece of market intelligence is the growth and cost improvement levels within your own business. Adding a micro element to the definition of market movement helps you understand more intimately the factors driving your business environment.

A micro economic understanding of your market begins with gathering information on commodity-specific growth rates. This information provides you with a gauge of what the potential leverage opportunities could or should have been had the information been recognized. Through this understanding, growth-related cost structure improvements within the commodity supply base could have been obtained. Mapped against these growth rates should be the average price improvement obtained during that period in each of the same commodity groupings. Finally, this information should be distilled down to the supplier level to measure growth versus performance.

Figure 6.2 represents industry data on historic commodity growth and cost savings trends. This information demonstrates a mismatch between the achieved savings levels and new business opportunities. Referring to the ACT process, where ACTs may have been used during initial sourcing, the organic commodity growth opportunity not captured in continuing cost savings would make it appropriate to reestablish the price baseline.

Figure 6.2 demonstrates some revealing commodity planning issues. The chart pairs growth patterns for three commodities with savings patterns for the same. The commodity with the highest aggregate spend, and demonstrating a 51 percent growth over the five-year period, showed the lowest savings. The commodity with the lowest total buy had the highest savings trend.

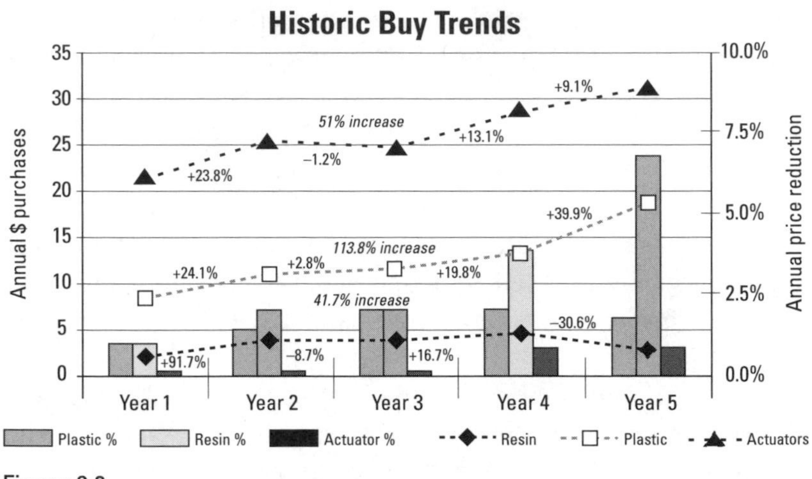

Figure 6.2

And the commodity with the highest growth pattern—over 110 percent—had the mid-level of savings. There needs to be a lot of research into these patterns, but at a minimum they demonstrate that the procurement team did not capture the volume efficiencies in the sourcing growth. The high savings in the low-growth commodity would tend to reflect a dynamic market influence, perhaps related to overcapacity issues, etc.

Micro evaluation also helps determine whether appropriate efforts have been historically made, or the appropriate levels of improvement achieved. Figure 6.3 shows a Pareto of commodity expenditures for a given fiscal year, with the associated savings percentages achieved in that period. This real-world example demonstrated that the efforts were being focused on the wrong commodities in working toward cost improvement. In the development of the price benchmark targets, these factors need to be taken into consideration in addressing the market factors.

WHAT TO BENCHMARK AND HOW TO BENCHMARK

Assessing the market movements is not the only objective in price benchmarking. A procurement organization also needs to

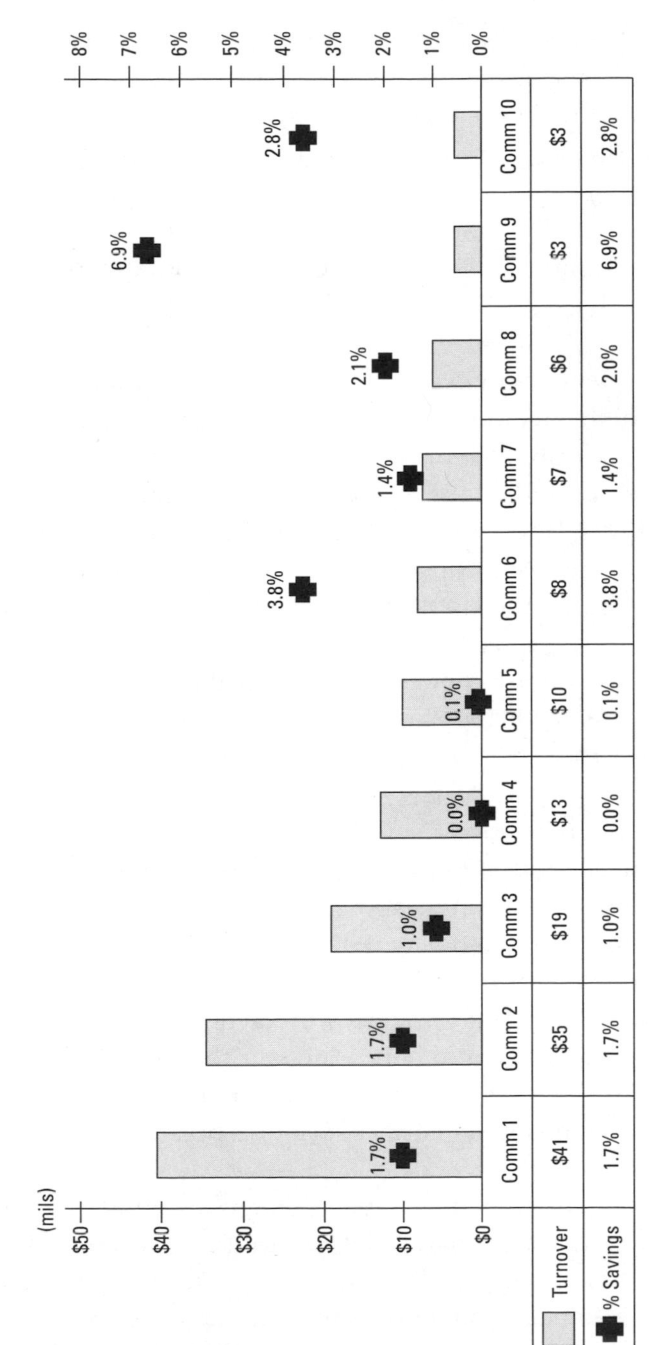

	Comm 1	Comm 2	Comm 3	Comm 4	Comm 5	Comm 6	Comm 7	Comm 8	Comm 9	Comm 10
Turnover	$41	$35	$19	$13	$10	$8	$7	$6	$3	$3
% Savings	1.7%	1.7%	1.0%	0.0%	0.1%	3.8%	1.4%	2.0%	6.9%	2.8%

Figure 6.3

consider how to respond to a supplier's (or suppliers') inability to meet the actual or perceived market changes. Many, if not most, buying companies are small or mid-cap-sized tier-two or below organizations, which usually do not possess natural supply leverage and are unable to demand market conformance. The ability to create leverage generally lies in the opportunities to source, or, more important here, to re-source business.

For price benchmarking to be effective, the quoting organizations (which include the incumbent supplier[s]) need to recognize not only the pure market shift in cost and supply structure, but also the understanding that a competitive assessment is the primary determinant of future (or continued) sourcing. Supporting the creation of this competitive environment is the appropriate selection of the universe of parts. During the price benchmarking process, the majority of parts selected must generally be those that are the simplest to manufacture, with the simplest tooling line-ups, and that are the easiest to move.

Simplicity is needed to facilitate any re-sourcing of parts and relocation of production tooling to a new supplier. Where part and tooling complexity is too high, the ability to re-source is greatly diminished, and with it, the actual or perceived power of negotiation leverage is also diminished. The seriousness with which the supply base perceives the actions and potential outcomes is almost entirely dependent on the ability to substitute parts or suppliers. Every event of the realization of an empty threat exponentially diminishes leverage potential.

The how-to of benchmarking is fairly straightforward. The acquisition team prepares the list of these easy-to-make or resource parts, gathers detailed tooling lineups for each part, prepares a standard quote package with target prices identified, and delivers it to the chosen suppliers. With the standard package, the team includes a description of the effort, the options to which the suppliers should quote (single parts or package quotes), and the actions to be taken upon quote recapitulation (recap). The rest is up to the suppliers.

Generally, the first commodity addressed in this way faces the most challenges of being taken seriously by the supply base. This is often due to the lack of preparation by the SCM organization in communicating a strategy that does not ring of a flavor of the month, but one that is actually part of a broader process. Once the news of the organization's efforts travels between suppliers, the subsequent commodity efforts proceed with much greater ease.

RECAPPING THE RESULTS

The results from the benchmarking study are not cherry picking the lowest price sources, but balancing cost, capabilities, and supply base planning. Supplier selection in price benchmarking should be seen as the first step in a consolidated supply base strategy. Using competitiveness in an aggregate sense across a multitude of parts establishes the future benchmark levels for ongoing supply competency. With supplier price attributes understood, SCM efforts can move forward to cost containment and capabilities.

Figure 6.4 shows the typical data consolidation from a price benchmarking recap. The key features are recognizing the total savings by sourcing to the lowest cost supplier in all cases (maximum savings) as well as the savings by selective sourcing. The selective sourcing can be based on the new incumbent supplier prices only (minimum savings), a new source total package price, or other decision-model-based choices. Figure 6.4 represents the results from an actual price benchmark study with minimum savings represented by incumbent pricing analysis.

Price Benchmarking—Commodity 1 Components

Part	Supplier	Pts/yr	Bal. out	$/100	Target	Supp 1	Supp 2	Supp 3	Supp 4	Max sav	Min sav
52159	Supp 3	50150	2005	185.00	172.00	n.q.	178.00	185.00	n.q.	3,511	0
52160	Supp 3	50200	2005	185.00	172.00	n.q.	178.00	185.00	n.q.	3,514	0
52161	Supp 3	31550	2005	195.00	180.00	n.q.	185.00	195.35	n.q.	3,155	0
52162	Supp 3	32500	2005	195.00	180.00	n.q.	185.00	195.35	n.q.	3,250	0
52169	Supp 3	48550	2002	165.00	149.00	165.00	n.q.	165.00	n.q.	0	0
52170	Supp 3	46900	2002	165.00	149.00	165.00	n.q.	165.00	n.q.	0	0
52239	Supp 3	73950	2009	199.80	180.00	199.00	198.00	199.80	n.q.	1,331	0
52240	Supp 3	70550	2009	199.80	180.00	199.00	198.00	199.80	n.q.	1,270	0
52287	Supp 3	180000	2009	177.90	149.00	172.00	159.00	161.00	n.q.	34,020	30,420
52288	Supp 3	180000	2009	177.90	149.00	172.00	159.00	161.00	n.q.	34,020	30,420
50372	Supp 4	230000	2006	142.00	120.00	n.q.	125.00	120.00	128.75	50,600	30,475
52061	Supp 4	32000	2009	174.60	152.00	207.00	152.00	156.50	163.30	7,232	3,616
52062	Supp 4	31000	2009	174.60	152.00	207.00	152.00	156.50	163.30	7,006	3,503
52301	Supp 4	424500	2009	174.60	152.00	160.00	158.00	159.60	163.30	70,467	47,968
52301	Supp 4	424500	2009	174.60	152.00	160.00	158.00	159.60	163.30	70,467	47,968
52067	Supp 1	230000	2006	205.00	165.00	200.00	170.00	180.90	n.q.	80,500	11,500
52098	Supp 1	230000	2006	205.00	165.00	200.00	175.00	183.00	n.q.	69,000	11,500
52099	Supp 1	33000	2006	223.00	165.00	218.00	170.00	184.50	n.q.	17,490	1,650
52100	Supp 1	33000	2006	223.00	165.00	218.00	170.00	184.50	n.q.	17,490	1,650
54425	Supp 1	270000	2004	296.50	252.00	288.00	n.q.	297.30	n.q.	22,950	22,950
54426	Supp 1	200000	2004	295.50	252.00	288.00	n.q.	297.30	n.q.	15,000	15,000
51053	Supp 2	105000	2004	211.00	186.00	n.q.	198.00	186.00	n.q.	26,250	13,650
52009	Supp 2	265000	2004	180.00	165.00	207.00	180.00	186.80	n.q.	0	0
52010	Supp 2	180000	2004	170.00	170.00	188.00	170.00	181.10	n.q.	0	0
52117	Supp 2	83150	2003	146.87	145.00	184.00	146.87	162.70	n.q.	0	0
52118	Supp 2	79700	2003	146.99	145.00	184.00	146.99	162.70	n.q.	0	0
52289	Supp 2	48800	2006	184.75	162.00	189.00	184.75	183.60	n.q.	561	0
52290	Supp 2	33350	2006	186.50	162.00	189.00	186.50	183.60	n.q.	967	0
52292	Supp 2	16400	2006	186.50	162.00	189.00	186.50	183.60	n.q.	476	0
54373	Supp 2	41300	2006	178.50	156.00	172.00	178.50	177.40	n.q.	2,685	0
54374	Supp 2	41650	2006	178.50	156.00	172.00	178.50	177.40	n.q.	2,707	0
54375	Supp 2	7550	2006	178.50	156.00	172.00	178.50	201.30	n.q.	491	0
54376	Supp 2	8100	2006	178.50	156.00	172.00	178.50	201.30	n.q.	527	0
54457	Supp 2	48550	2002	240.00	199.00	226.00	240.00	247.40	n.q.	6,797	0
54458	Supp 2	46900	2002	240.00	199.00	226.00	240.00	247.40	n.q.	6,566	0
52018	Supp 5	86900	2005	86.00	85.00	n.q.	n.q.	83.40	n.q.	2,259	0
										Max. saving	**Min. saving**
									1st Year Savings	**562,558**	**272,271**

Figure 6.4 Price Benchmarking Results

CASE STUDY 6.2

Questions

1. In pursuing the immediate cost savings, what steps did DSW initially take with its suppliers—that is, what alternatives did they have to choose from?
2. What could the anticipated level of success be with each of the possibilities identified in question 1?
3. What steps would the DSW supply chain executive need to take with respect to maintaining a future focus?

Answers

1. One of DSW's operating groups set aside its SCM effort and pursued a "scorched earth policy," which included with universal price concession demands, massive market test and resource efforts, and some unilateral demands.

   A second operating group followed a price benchmarking exercise, establishing market-based ACTs for nearly 65 percent of its total buy (# of parts, not $).
2. The first group achieved a gross savings level of approximately 5.5 percent. Netted from that was approximately 1.25 percent for tooling adaptation costs, recertification costs, etc., for a net total of 4.25 percent. Supplier relations were greatly deteriorated.

   The second group achieved a gross savings level of 8 percent on those commodities that used the price benchmarking process. There were not incremental tooling or certification charges, as the quote package required that these costs must be borne by the supplier as part of the sourcing package. Only approximately 5 percent of the total parts quoted required any resourcing efforts. The net savings on total dollar buy basis was 6.25 percent.

3. DSW's supply chain executive needed to consolidate the various operating unit procurement activities to follow a single business process path. The market cost factors were captured on only a portion of the total buy, requiring a re-verification on the missing parts. With this information, DSW could move on to other cost and capabilities evaluations.

7

Phase III: Short-Term Process Improvement

MOVING FROM THE MARKET TO THE PLANT

Examining each of the value chain cost elements in a sequenced manner provides the broadest evaluation and control of total product cost. In many cases the efforts in SCM fail to recognize the importance, and significance, that the manufacturing processes and efficiencies play in overall cost containment and control. Phase III of the crisis improvement plan uses this approach, and more fully adopts lean practices into the SCM process.

The adaptation of the lean manufacturing techniques in this phase is the use of point kaizen efforts. The application of point kaizen will be explored in greater detail later, but the term generally applies to process improvements made to distinct processes around a contained production cell. While kaizen usually implies slow systematic improvement, I have included it in the kaikaku elements as this particular application strives for immediate and significant improvement in a radical way. Womak, et al. say that radical improvement is a key element to quick success: "You'll need a change agenda plus the core of lean knowledge (not necessarily from the same person), some type of crisis to serve as a lever for change, a map of your value streams, and a determination to kaikaku quickly to your value-creating activities in order to produce rapid results which your organization can't ignore."[1]

CASE STUDY 7.1

Process-based improvement efforts were not new to DSW. There was an ingrained philosophy of continuous improvement in the manufacturing environment. This process was exclusively an internal one, and had not yet been taken to the supply base. In preparing for a launch of these efforts with the suppliers, trained lean implementers were permanently assigned to the SCM team.

Questions

1. In preparing for the launch of the process improvement program with suppliers, what key elements did the lean implementers need to take into consideration?
2. How would DSW establish its credibility with suppliers with respect to the ability to identify and implement change?
3. How would DSW capture the savings opportunities to realize the immediate savings opportunities?

PHASE III — SHORT-TERM PROCESS IMPROVEMENT (SPI) PROCEDURE

Definition

SPI's emphasis is to obtain the most process-based improvements with the least amount of expenditure in the shortest period of time. There is a beginning and an end to each event,

1. Womak and Jones, *Lean Thinking,* p. 247

with a focus on specific manufacturing processes or suppliers. Using a point-kaizen-based effort; the program focuses its efforts on suppliers who exhibit the following traits:

- A lack of neatness and orderliness, poor and insufficient measures of productivity, high scrap rates in excess of industry standards, or excessive inspection indicating a process that is out of control.
- Suppliers exhibiting significant process-based opportunities, unprepared to fully implement lean manufacturing systems. In such a case, time spent training the supplier to implement lean manufacturing principles could be a non-valued-added use of time. However, the opportunities for short-term gain should not be overlooked. (This would distinguish point kaizen efforts from flow kaizen efforts.)
- Business levels insufficient to warrant a full flow kaizen implementation, yet exhibiting opportunity on current parts supplied. For example, if each kaizen event costs approximately $30,000 (travel, time, training, etc.), the payback (or ROI) should exceed the total cost by four or five times. Many suppliers who demonstrate improvement opportunities may not have a $100,000 potential. This mechanism captures that opportunity, using the least amount of expenditures possible by creating a larger and/or viable ROI. For example: a supplier providing $2,000,000 in annual sales with a 50 percent material cost, 30 percent fixed OH and profit, leaves 20 percent or $400,000 to the effects of SPI. If you achieve a 20 percent productivity improvement on the manufacturing cost basis, the potential savings is $80,000.
- Have been identified by the buyer or SDE (supplier development engineer) as having good and/or great potential in a certain area of their process. Again, this could be based on a supplier's cost structure or process as compared to other comparable suppliers.

Implementation procedure

SPI is a highly focused approach on a limited number of processes at a given time, usually one, no more than two. The process contains three stages, which will take a total of approximately one month to complete. Each of these is discussed in the following sections.

Stage I: Identification and Preparation (3 days)

The acquisition team reviews the lean manufacturing and SPI objectives with the lean facilitators. Taking into consideration the factors for SPI potential candidates, a list is developed based on the results of a supplier brainstorming process. This list is broken down into kaizen and SPI potential suppliers. From that list a proposed timeline is developed based on available resources. The three days necessary for this can be identified as follows:

- *Day 1:* Brainstorming session, potential candidate list development.
- *Day 2:* Schedule development, prioritization based on resources.
- *Day 3:* Buyer contacts suppliers' management, gets buy-in to conduct SPI.

Stage II: Implementation (1 week)

During this phase, the company's and supplier's team members implement an accelerated version of point kaizen. The key here is that the team develops and agrees on the measurables of productivity and stays focused to the intent of SPI—that is, short-term focus on a specific portion of a process. If the team identifies broader opportunities they may extend their length of the stay and perform several SPIs as needed. A typical event would consist of the following events by day:

- *Day 1:* Kickoff meeting. Obtain information on historical productivity measurements, lean manufacturing knowledge base, operator brainstorming, brief lean manufacturing workshop and training session, and review line in operation.

- *Day 2:* Establish baseline calculations and prioritization of brainstorming session. Move to line for detailed analysis and review, keeping brainstorming ideas at hand. Establish prioritization of implementation. Implement first two to three ideas, monitor and evaluate changes.
- *Day 3:* Measure productivity as pieces per operator hour to capture throughput and labor efficiencies. Analyze scrap data, compare to prior process to ensure equal or better performance.
- *Day 4:* Continue to measure productivity. Consider implementing one to two more ideas if possible. If productivity measurements are not clear at this point, do not try to implement additional changes.
- *Day 5:* Review final measurements of productivity, agree on the results (including total financial impact) and jointly publish a report using the lean manufacturing process summaries. Review, follow up ideas, set dates for completion, and assign responsibility for reporting and documenting those results.

Stage III: Closure

During this part of the process we want to accomplish two key items. One is to document the results of the SPI event. Two is to initiate a purchase order amendment to input the applicable price reduction. In the introduction and launch of this program, your company needs to define the savings sharing mechanism. For example, a program may equally divide the savings 50/50 based on total savings identified. The supplier may then be given one of three options: do nothing and equally divide the savings; implement savings ideas without assistance; or implement the savings with the assistance of your lean facilitators.

Generally, kaizen initiated savings have some slippage in the gained efficiencies. This reality may enter into the discussion on the division of savings, or postimplementation recovery. However, since the definition of total savings is based on concurrence of the total savings potential, there usually already exists some extra savings not captured in the reported and divided amount.

Ideally, stage III should be completed within one week of the conclusion of stage I. If this is not accomplished, you risk losing the focus on the implementation of the efforts, as well as the savings opportunities identified by your SPI program.

KAIZEN VERSUS SPI

Although point kaizen techniques are being employed here, the process is identified as short-term profit improvement for a very specific reason. Kaizen is an institutionalized element of a broader lean philosophy that is championed in a top-down fashion, but implemented as a bottom-up process. In implementing point kaizen efficiencies, the people think, eat, and sleep lean, continually generating improvement ideas. For living kaizen to be effective, all levels of management must buy in to the underlying lean philosophy, not only in verse but in their actions.

SPI on the other hand is a process that is both implemented and championed top down. In some applications of this kind of short-term effort, the program may force-feed process if necessary. General Motors' program PICOS[2] is clearly an example of a force-fed SPI program, whereas Chrysler's SCORE[3] program was not. This was an effort where the operators and/or supplier

2. PICOS was a process improvement program utilized by General Motors in the late 1980's and early 1990's. The process was a "stand-alone" effort, not coordinated with any other lean efforts.
3. SCORE was a total cost savings program utilized by Chrysler Corporation prior to its acquisition by Daimler. This program generated all types of savings ideas, usually offered by the suppliers, and jointly implemented with Chrysler. At the time, SCORE was viewed as the model for all automotive industry supplier suggestion programs.

themselves may not have been brought into the entire process, but where GM process experts made the changes, documented the results, and reported the savings. The application of SPI outlined here is not intended to be a force-fed process. By using the point kaizen disciplines, SPI engages the suppliers in a participative effort designed to deliver mutual improvement. While SPI may not necessarily represent a fundamental plant or company-wide paradigm shift to lean techniques, it can provide the basis of change in that direction.

CASE STUDY 7.2

Questions

1. In preparing for the launch of the process improvement program with suppliers, what key elements did the lean implementers need to take into consideration?
2. How would DSW establish its credibility with suppliers with respect to the ability to identify and implement change?
3. How would DSW capture the savings opportunities to realize the immediate savings opportunities?

Answers

1. The issue of credibility was the main consideration that needed to be made in the application of SPI with the suppliers. Past experience for the suppliers led them to be skeptical of any cooperative effort. By building this effort as part of an integrated supply strategy, the acceptance of the work was greater than expected.

   Also, significant preparation needed to be made in training the participants in the application of the tools and techniques in use for the SPI effort. The order of tasks and timing of implementation needed to remain per plan without variation to provide for program integrity.

2. The primary credibility was established through DSW's own internal implementation of point kaizen efforts. Lean techniques had become the method of business for DSW throughout its international facilities. By conducting a portion of the orientation of both the internal and supplier teams at DSW "model" locations, the suppliers were able to view implementation, progress, and sustained improvement. While SPI was not intended to be a fully integrated lean effort, its roots are from the point kaizen lean integration efforts.

3. The savings were captured through an immediate 50/50 split of the documented net line savings potential. Purchase order reductions were taken, with implementation support available as needed. In some cases, the supplier savings portions were applied to previously committed, but not yet obtained, price reductions. The effort resulted in a net 3.5 percent cumulative first year savings on total buy, with actions occurring over a nine-month period.

8

Phase IV: Value Analysis/ Value Engineering

THE BEGINNING OF THE KAIZEN EFFORTS

From the beginning of this book the importance of maintaining a view to the future has been repeatedly stressed. The need to balance short- and long-term cost and price improvements has been highlighted. In phase IV of the crisis improvement, the transition to the longer-term horizon begins to take place.

Value analysis and value engineering (VA/VE) moves the cost evaluation to the next logical place in the value stream: design. Depending on your industry, design-based cost improvements can either be an easy and quick introduction or encompass a lengthy validation and prove-out effort. Value analysis generally refers to design refinements to existing production components, whereas value engineering means designing improvements into new products based on cost and other performance objectives. In our crisis scenario, the efforts focus on VA only. Some of the design opportunities can be captured and incorporated into next generation VE efforts, but those will not bear out the immediate savings required in a crisis.

CASE STUDY 8.1

Value analysis and value engineering was a formalized process at DWS. Led by its engineering organization, DSW supplemented its supplier-based material cost improvement by targeting specified levels of VA/VE savings. The VA/VE task was divided by product category and operational unit, giving specific goals to each of the engineering managers. The value of the annual target was based upon a gap analysis derived from the shortfall of annual plan known savings to required profit levels.

Supplier participation in the DSW VA/VE effort was by request, and typically involved raw material utilization versus component part change participation. Much of the resistance to supplier participation concerned the proper crediting to VA results (i.e., who would get the credit for the savings).

Questions

1. What other factors may have limited supplier involvement in DSW's VA/VE effort?
2. How could or should DSW begin to engage its suppliers in this effort? What expectations may the suppliers hold with respect to participating in VA/VE?
3. Could the internal DSW VA process gain any improvements through observing supplier participation in VA/VE or in their own programs?

Definition

VA/VE is a planned, clean-sheet approach to problem solving, focusing on specific design and process characteristics. Value analysis is used to improve value after the start of production, whereas value engineering is used during the initial product design phase before costly expenditures are incurred. The scope of the application can go from a single process, or program, to multiple programs involving the supplier's design-driven processes and operations.

Typical applications would include:

1. Raw material flexibility.
2. Stalled process changes.
3. Tolerancing and specification relief.
4. Processing flexibility.
5. Post start-of-production reviews.

Implementation Procedure

There are three unique approaches to the VA/VE process with the supplier. They are supplier based, commodity based, and ongoing. Each of these is discussed in the following sections.

Supplier based. This is a highly focused, kaikaku style approach to VA/VE. Conducted either at a supplier's location or other off-site location, this event typically lasts three to four days. Included in this multiple-day design review would be the following agenda:

- *Conduct process review.* This review should cover the supplier's processes that are specifically driven by part design characteristics. This review is not a point kaizen process effort, but an evaluation of the link between design and manufacturing.
- *Brainstorm design alternatives.* This activity should include participants representing a diverse cross section of functional expertise. Sometimes called BrainTeaming,™[1] this

1. BrainTeaming™ is a proprietary approach to group problem solving developed by Value Innovations, Ltd. Information regarding BrainTeaming™ and Value Innovations, Ltd. can be found at *www.innovatevalue.com.*

group-based problem-solving approach provides the greatest degree of input and creativity in balancing design, manufacturing, and commercial needs.

- *Prioritize the ideas.* The prioritization effort can be based on ease of implementation, impact of cost savings, simplicity of product validation, or any other characteristic. The choice of the prioritization factor should be driven by the integration factors to the rest of the business or SCM plan being implemented.
- *Review similar processes.* This step is to capture the lessons learned from the initial VA effort and apply them in the greatest scope possible. It can be from this step that VE considerations affecting operations can be taken into account for the next-generation project.
- *Return visits.* As required, the VA team should return to the supplier location as a follow-up to the initially generated VA idea list. Although potential new ideas should be explored, the team's primary focus should be the full implementation of the initial ideas and driving these ideas through the approval system.

Commodity based. Commodity-based VA/VE is a concentrated effort focused on a specific commodity or commodity subgroup, rather than on a single supplier. The campaign is designed to take one week to generate and define the ideas. Three to four suppliers that would like to participate in this program are selected based on current technology mix, long-term agreements, and history with your company. Commodity-based efforts include the following stages:

- *Stage 1.* The first three to four days of the week will follow the agenda below for each of the selected suppliers. The final day of the week your company's participants will meet and review all of the gathered ideas.
- *Stage 2.* All of the commodity suppliers will receive a package identifying the ideas from their buyer. Each supplier

will need to calculate the cost reduction, for them, associated for each of the identified ideas.

- *Stage 3*. You then prioritize the ideas, selecting the first five to ten to start the implementation process. As each of the ideas are completed, the next one on the list will be started until all of the feasible ideas are implemented.

Agenda

8:00 am– 8:15 am	Introduction/Review agenda
8:15 am– 9:00 am	Competitive analysis review (if avail.)
9:00 am–11:30 am	Review elements of cost 1. material 2. design 3. processing 4. labor 5. overhead 6. scrap
Brainstorming	Comparison to similar products/processes
11:30 am–12:30 pm	Working lunch
12:30 pm– 2:30 pm	Evaluate ideas; Establish theoretical costs
2:30 pm– 3:00 pm	Fill out VA forms
3:00 pm– 4:00 pm	Prioritize ideas

Ongoing. The third option is not a concentrated program, but rather a continuous process. This process provides a significant opportunity for the development of VE actions. There are five categories that ongoing supplier VA requests would generally fall into. They are:

1. *Raw material flexibility*. Raw material flexibility involves situations in which suppliers are required to validate individual raw material suppliers on specific raw material brands. Often a supplier's standard practices would allow the use of a broader supplier base or material selection. Often driven by customer suggestions or demands or in place because of convenience, specific materials and suppliers are specified versus performance characteristics of the part or material. Material flexibility targets this issue

and "un-paints" the supply organization from its corner of single source only.

2. *Stalled process changes.* Most organizations contain a process change procedure managed either through its technical or operational staff for the purpose of managing internal and external change requests. In instances where a supplier has requested a process change through these normal channels, and that change is either stalled or has been denied without justification, a supplier should submit a VA request. The VA request refocuses the organization's change management efforts to correspond with the cost crisis at hand. While not necessarily designed to replace the standard process, the VA submission approach helps relieve the system of convenient back-shelving of ideas considered to be of low priority by engineering.
3. *Tolerancing and specification relief.* All industries have seen overengineering efforts put in place to address specific, but often historic or anecdotal problems. Driven to correct some perceived performance problems, designers often specify part performance characteristics in excess of normal parameters. The effect is to introduce significant inspection and detections costs within a supplier's operation. Focused supplier development and improvement activities provide for significantly improved process performance to 5, 6, and even 7 sigma,[2] providing statistically reliable and repeatable processes. When a supplier can demonstrate that its process is in control and that the process mean is centered (or that the process would not be 4 to 6 sigma capable even if the mean was centered), then the supplier should request a change. There are two

2. Six sigma performance relates to the number of standard distributions around the mean (or targeted) specification requirement. Each increase in standard distribution results in significantly reduced reject levels. At six sigma the approximate reject rate for the specified process/characteristic would be 6 PPM (parts per million).

avenues for the supplier to pursue in this situation. The first option is a drawing change request. This works best for single components. The second option is a VA request. This works best for families of parts or when the first avenue has been tried and denied without sufficient justification.

4. *Processing flexibility.* Non-value-added costs have been introduced to many suppliers through regulating their processing flexibility with the validation requirements. There are many industries where banks of identical machinery are used interchangeably to run production. In some cases the need to constrain the process to a single machine or to only qualified machines is justified, but there are other cases where it is not. The elimination of process inflexibility can contribute to a significant savings potential by freeing up machining capacity utilization plans, and through the optimization of available labor.
5. *Post start-of-production reviews.* Program management processes provide for milestone reviews at which critical program or product issues are reviewed at key phases during development and launch. Often ignored are the issues identified during the launch and ramp-up phases of product introduction. Often, program teams have already been disbanded or reassigned by the time full production is in place. The issues identified during launch provide the basis for significant VA potential. A module (assembly) or part-level design review may occur after the start of production. Suppliers who manufacture the major assembly components are invited to come together to review issues that have arisen since the start of production. A supplier VA team would be formed, or the program development team would be reconstituted for the effort to facilitate a system review. This program-specific review process allows for the immediate capture and potential implementation of lessons learned during a program production launch phase.

MAKING THE PROCESS WORK

The primary challenge in the development and implementation of a VA/VE effort is designing the process by which suggestions are submitted, processed, and approved. This effort is no small challenge. In introducing a VA/VE process, limited resources that are engaged in other activities are asked to redirect their efforts to cover ground they feel has already been addressed. Also affecting the processes' ability to function properly are the personal effects and attitudes that individuals or groups face when forced to recognize that the initial design and development efforts may not have been the best.

Figure 8.1 demonstrates the complexity in simply designing a new supplier-based VA/VE effort. The various process flows show the multiple functions, reviews, and evaluations necessary in implementing a VA program. The flow through the process requires involvement, forms, and systems from engineering; purchasing; suppliers; manufacturing; finance; technical services (testing); and others. Monthly status reviews and implementation progress reviews must occur to ensure continued performance.

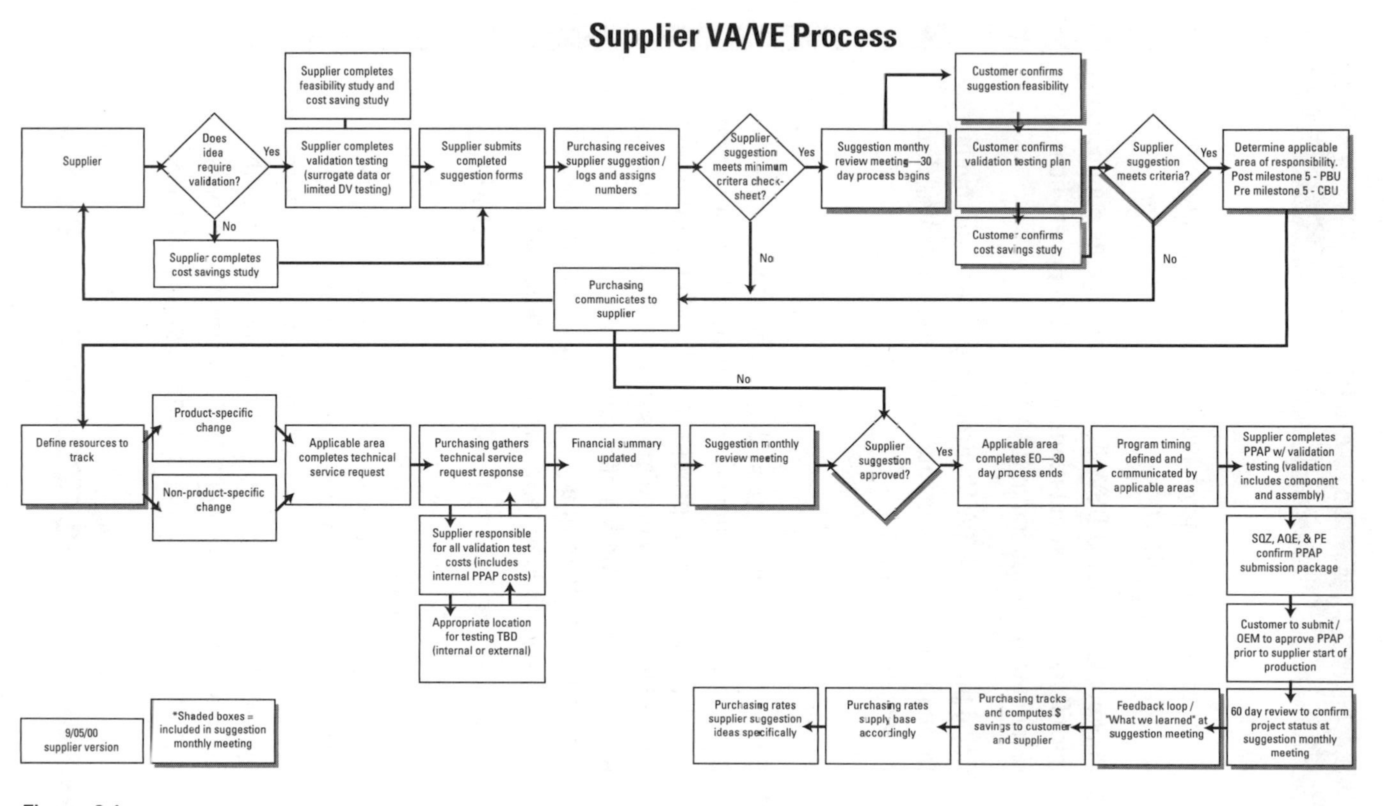

Supplier VA/VE Process
Supplier
Does idea require validation?
Yes
No
Supplier completes cost savings study
Supplier completes feasibility study and cost saving study
Supplier completes validation testing (surrogate data or limited DV testing)
Supplier submits completed suggestion forms
Purchasing receives supplier suggestion / logs and assigns numbers
Supplier suggestion meets minimum critera check-sheet?
Yes
No
Suggestion monthy review meeting—30 day process begins
Customer confirms suggestion feasibility
Customer confirms validation testing plan
Customer confirms cost savings study
Supplier suggestion meets criteria?
Yes
No
Determine applicable area of responsibility. Post milestone 5 - PBU Pre milestone 5 - CBU
Purchasing communicates to supplier
No
Define resources to track
Product-specific change
Non-product-specific change
Applicable area completes technical service request
Purchasing gathers technical service request response
Supplier responsible for all validation test costs (includes internal PPAP costs)
Appropriate location for testing TBD (internal or external)
Financial summary updated
Suggestion monthly review meeting
Supplier suggestion approved?
Yes
Applicable area completes EO—30 day process ends
Program timing defined and communicated by applicable areas
Supplier completes PPAP w/ validation testing (validation includes component and assembly)
SQZ, AQE, & PE confirm PPAP submission package
Customer to submit / OEM to approve PPAP prior to supplier start of production
60 day review to confirm project status at suggestion monthly meeting
Feedback loop / "What we learned" at suggestion meeting
Purchasing tracks and computes $ savings to customer and supplier
Purchasing rates supply base accordingly
Purchasing rates supplier suggestion ideas specifically
9/05/00 supplier version
*Shaded boxes = included in suggestion monthly meeting

Figure 8.1

CASE STUDY 8.2

Questions

1. What other factors may have limited supplier involvement in DSW's VA/VE effort?
2. How could or should DSW begin to engage its suppliers in this effort? What expectations may the suppliers hold with respect to participating in VA/VE?
3. Could the internal DSW VA process gain any improvements through observing supplier participation in VA/VE or in their own programs?

Answers

1. DSW did not have in place the mechanism by which suppliers could submit suggestions, or by which suggestions could be evaluated, processed, or implemented, nor a method for applying credit to supplier efforts. The recognition of this required a significant amount of work to move the VA/VE efforts from a program to a process (i.e., short-term efforts to a long-term sustaining process).
2. DSW was able to engage its suppliers in the VA process by building the traditional material savings strategy into a total cost management activity.

   While the appearance may have been initially received as a no-choice proposition, it was based upon and reflected the changing industry dynamics of total cost management. The suppliers were given commodity- and supplier-specific targets, with performance monitored against these (and other) criteria. A portion of the savings was retained by the supplier, with the remainder applied to their annual target objectives.

3. By designing and implementing a supplier suggestion program similar to the one outlined in Figure 8.1, DSW recognized the need to more fully manage the process through monthly reviews. By evaluating new and existing ideas, DSW could ensure that the pipeline for ideas remained full. DSW was also able to monitor the submission to implementation rate and work toward moving the noise of bad ideas out of the system. By monitoring specific supplier performance, the DSW supplier development and procurement team could assist suppliers who appeared either unable or unwilling to contribute to the design-based improvements.

9

Phase V: Lean Manufacturing

MOVING OUT OF CRISIS—SUPPLIER-BASED LEAN MANUFACTURING

Moving toward lean manufacturing practices and systems in the suppliers' operations represents the final phase of the crisis plan. This final phase, however, does not end, is not a program, and represents a fundamental shift in business management. Lean-based manufacturing, usually exemplified by the use of Toyota Production System (TPS) methodologies, takes the art of kaizen to a different level. Whereas we've so far discussed kaizen as an event, lean efforts transform kaizen to a process encompassing the entire business enterprise. This concept creates flow kaizen where the flow of material, information, design, manufacturing, and administration are all parts of continuous improvement efforts.

Taking lean disciplines to the supply base requires practical experience and knowledgeable facilitators from your organization. Academic understanding of lean systems is by no means sufficient to begin an implementation effort with the suppliers. The information in this chapter defines just one of many methodologies of beginning a lean enterprise implementation plan for the suppliers. The important lesson here is that there needs to be a well-thought-out, and, even more important, well-executed deployment of lean. Without planning and execution perfection, the credibility of the practice and of the facilitators comes into question. The lean practice never becomes an institutionalized business approach.

The following lean SCM definition is a simplified version for the purposes of introducing the concept to SCM professionals. *Lean Thinking*, by Womack and Jones is an excellent resource for more fully defining lean and lean efforts, including kaikaku approaches. Particularly appropriate for this section is a quote from *Lean Thinking* regarding the "radical path." "There is an alternative, radical path to perfection, a total value stream kaikaku involving all the firms from start to finish."[1] It is exactly such an approach I am speaking of when I recommend supplier lean implementation as part of an SCM strategy.

Definition

Lean manufacturing is a continuous improvement program taken in small steps. It improves the process by eliminating waste, standardizing work, and creating flexible manufacturing. It is typically focused on the production process, working to evolve it, rather than just change it. Typical tools used to achieve this improvement include: line smoothing, the Five Ss (sort, set in order, shine, standardize, sustain), cycle time reduction, and work area reconfiguration. The application of Toyota Production System (TPS) or similar methodologies is also used.

Implementation Procedure

The lean manufacturing program is a highly focused tool deployed with a limited number of suppliers at a given time. Within each supplier a pilot or showcase line is chosen for the implementation of lean. The process can be viewed as happen-

1. Womack and Jones, *Lean Thinking*, p. 91.

CASE STUDY 9.1

DSW had already implemented lean methodologies in its own manufacturing operations throughout the world. The implementation, however, had been one of internal focus only. The supply chain had not been tapped for its ability to support the lean effort. Lean facilitators had been trained and deployed throughout the company. DSW's SCM group had recently acquired four lean facilitators throughout its worldwide SCM operations.

In developing its strategic initiatives, the SCM group was struggling with the best way to deploy these resources. The advent of the crisis situation complicated this deployment question, as these very knowledgeable and experienced resources were not provided the environment in which to fully utilize their skills.

Questions

1. Given the need to respond to the crisis situation, how should DSW deploy its lean SCM resources? In what way could the lean facilitators contribute to the crisis plan?
2. When deploying lean initiatives with its suppliers, in what area should DSW focus its initial efforts?
3. Why would DSW want to deploy lean with its suppliers? What advantage can be gained in QCD (quality, cost, delivery) from these lean efforts?

ing in two waves. Each wave contains three phases. The first wave will take approximately one year to "complete."[2]

---

2. "Complete" is enclosed in quotation marks as it is an accepted understanding within lean deployment that no process is actually ever complete, but phases of improvement have been accomplished.

Wave One

Wave One is the aided implementation of lean manufacturing systems with primary suppliers, and usually encompasses complex or high value components. Critical to Wave One's success, and facilitating the ability to move to a second wave of implementation is capturing on learning both internally, and at the suppliers' locations.

Phase I: Developing the plan (three months). This phase is divided into three stages. Each stage is about one month in duration. Your company and the supplier need to work closely together during this phase. During Stage 1 your lean facilitators would have residence at the supplier location during Weeks 1 and 4. The facilitator's presence during Weeks 2 and 3 would be periodic based on the event's needs.

- ***Stage 1 (one month):***
  - *Week 1: Kick-off (one to three days).* The kick-off phase includes training the team in lean vocabulary, philosophy of lean in business, and methods improvement and measure, etc., baseline calculations of existing production (or other) operations and efficiencies; brainstorming changes as needed, and prioritization of implementation efforts.
  - *Week 2: Preparation (one to ten days).* This phase includes scheduling of implementation efforts, maintenance of facility and equipment in preparation for additional changes, ordering equipment and supplies, and whatever must be completed to start implementation.
  - *Week 3: Implementation (two to four days per implementation task).* Week 3 is the hands-on revision to the gemba (workplace) by implementing the lean changes. The length of the changes may significantly exceed this time period. Like all lean efforts, implementation really has no end, just continuous refinement.
  - *Week 4: Measure productivity (three to five days).* Lean efficiency measures are many; however, the most impor-

tant is the direct measure of manufacturing productivity. The definition of productivity is: output in pieces times 60 minutes divided by working hours times the number of operators. This and other efficiency measures defined in Week 1 need to be updated and reported. Hoshin planning and management by plan (MBP) are effective tools for monitoring and reporting progress toward objectives.

- ***Stage 2 (one month).*** During this stage we will evaluate the effects of the changes, improve the initial ideas, and reprioritize those ideas. The lean facilitators will have an on-site presence during this stage of approximately one week.
- ***Stage 3 (one month).*** This stage is for measuring productivity and reporting improvements. Lean facilitators will have an on-site presence of approximately one week. This time should be used by the executive team for a supportive review that is part of the hoshin/MBP process.

Phase II: Implementing the plan (nine months). This phase is divided into three stages, but unlike Phase I, the timing for each stage depends on each supplier's unique situation. Your presence during this stage would involve periodic one-day visits to support the supplier and monitor progress.

- ***Stage 1.*** This is the point at which the supplier begins to fully take the lead of the lean implementation efforts. The supplier continues to implement and deploy the next set of lean objectives. Efficiency gains are continually measured from the ongoing implementation and translated to cost improvements. These savings are reported back to the buyer as they are measured and verified.
- ***Stage 2.*** At Stage 2 in Phase II, the supplier has completed the initial implementation of lean practices of the targeted process (the pilot line or process) and now looks to apply the ideas and principles realized on the first effort to other processes. The supplier will report cost savings back to the customer's buyer as they are measured and verified.

- ***Stage 3.*** At this point the supplier has completed implementing the lean manufacturing process on similar processes and starts applying the program to other product lines and processes, and may include administrative as well as manufacturing processes.

Phase III: Learning and verifying results. Phase III is a formal supportive review by the supplier with the customer. The review is made to a cross-functional management group from those functions that normally interact with the supplier. Progress toward implementation, efficiency and cost improvements, roadblocks, and other issues are reviewed in detail with support assigned as necessary, including detailed continuation plans. Phase III also represents the transition to the next wave of application at the supplier.

Wave Two

Wave Two of the implementation of lean systems within the supply base focuses on two main elements. The first of these is to formally expand the lean initiatives beyond the manufacturing process at the Wave One suppliers. In this effort, the suppliers take a fresh look at the processes addressed in Phase I; examine the lessons learned; modify the process as necessary; and move to other functional operations.

Many six-sigma programs focus on the nonmanufacturing processes in effort to define and deliver improvements. Kaizen for administration is also a commonly deployed methodology used for this purpose.

MAKING SENSE OF LEAN

The definition and process identified here only skims the surface of the breadth of lean manufacturing and lean systems. To be able to utilize the process outlined above, your organization will require practical lean experience and education. The experiments that you make in implementing lean are best made within your four walls. Without this experience and education you will be unable to anticipate the suppliers' implementation issues and be unable to guide the supplier toward solutions.

A significant element included in the implementation process is the inclusion of specific measures of cost performance. While operational efficiency measures ultimately translate to cost and profit improvement, traditional lean measures do not include cost performance. Lean systems implementation (with suppliers) as part of a SCM effort uses specific cost measures as a primary element. With this measure, it becomes unfortunately easy to let lean become a cost savings program. By this I mean, the drive for cost improvements becomes the force leading lean implementation, not lean implementation defining cost improvement. In bringing together a total cost improvement plan, lean efficiencies become the ongoing ability to continuously achieve savings. It is these savings that ensure market competitiveness in the long term. This will be discussed more in Chapter 10.

CASE STUDY 9.2

Questions

1. Given the need to respond to the crisis situation, how should DSW deploy its lean SCM resources? In what way could the lean facilitators contribute to the crisis plan?

2 When deploying lean initiatives with its suppliers, in what area should DSW focus its initial efforts?

3. Why would DSW want to deploy lean with its suppliers? What advantage can be gained in QCD (quality, cost, delivery) from these lean efforts?

Answers

1. The lean resources were provided initially as a preparation force leading the development of the lean implementation plans. Building on their work as participants on the acquisition teams, the lean resources provided the continuity from the prior phases into the lean development effort. While the prior phase and lean preparation work didn't fully utilize the lean skills, the presence of additional human resources facilitated a sustained focus on cost improvement.

2. The initial focus of lean efforts was based a traditional Pareto analysis of spending. This technique was used throughout the crisis plan in prioritizing the commodities and suppliers within the commodities to which the efforts were going to be initially applied. In addition, it was with those suppliers who were deemed long term or to have long-term potential that lean efforts were deployed. Short-term or transitional suppliers were not included in the lean efforts.

3. DSW deployed its resources to its key suppliers to build a long-term efficiency plan, working to achieve productivity improvements. These efforts resulted in multifaceted cost improvement efforts through operational efficiency gains; reduced quality reject costs; and improved delivery and schedule attainment, resulting in ongoing cost improvements for DSW.

SECTION III

The Standard Environment

10

Defining the Standard Environment

Defining the standard environment is far more complex than defining the crisis environment as in Section II. The complexity is that because each industry provides for such a diverse business environment, standard becomes a relative term. For our purposes we will define standard as the traditional environment in which business is conducted. While the regular challenges and stresses of business still exist, the factors we previously described as crisis are not present. Also the standard environment provides some luxury of time. The ability to develop and implement business strategies and approaches is not unduly constrained by expediency.

The standard environment is also hallmarked by a broad focus on business systems and systems integration. Generally businesses manage their efforts and strategies through the development, implementation, and utilization of strategic planning methods. In the standard environment, SCM organizations work to support broader corporate strategies as well as developing unique supply chain strategies. This integration is key to achieving overall corporate objectives.

CASE STUDY 10.1

The supply chain efforts at DSW have had varying degrees of success throughout its various divisions. There has been a history of achieving cost improvements, supporting requirements determined by the company's corporate financial office. The various divisions pursued the required improvements through loosely coordinated efforts. Collectively, the SCM efforts in the divisions have delivered roughly 3 percent gross savings from previous pricing levels. Offsetting this savings is a 1 to 2 percent inflationary impact to commodity materials.

Questions

1. How would DSW determine if the SCM's contribution to the company's financial improvements was sufficient? What factors would or should DSW include in this evaluation?
2. What ways could the DSW SCM organization better coordinate its divisional efforts? How do these efforts vary depending on DSW's view on centralized or decentralized SCM?
3. Would DSW have any alternative in the way it manages inflationary effects on purchase content? How does the industry in which DSW operates affect the approach to inflationary effects?

HISTORY OF IMPROVEMENT

The standard environment in SCM also means that there exists an ongoing history of cost (and other QCD) improvements achieved through supply base management efforts. These savings may be limited, or spotty in nature, but represent evidence that some level of professional effort has been made. The importance in this is that we are not starting at ground zero.

Future efforts can focus on building upon the achievements and formulating new approaches based on what has been learned from the past (both bad and good).

Often the history of improvement is driven by the demands of groups outside of SCM. Generally, these demands come from the financial staff dictating a specific cost improvement level that must be obtained. This tactic is not necessarily bad and is often driven from the lack of commitment coming from the SCM organization. The vision must be the self-determination of the SCM organization. SCM must have the ability to predict the improvement levels that will be obtained, the market environment driving the changes, and the commercial parity with improvements in customer pricing. Learning from the improvement history and penning the future plan must drive this vision.

EFFORTS BUILT FROM STRATEGY

To achieve the greatest level of success, the efforts of the supply chain management group must be integrated with and supportive of broader corporate objectives. The ability to accomplish this lies in the methods in which SCM objectives are developed and implemented. Through strategic procurement and SCM implementation, these objectives can be identified and achieved.

Strategic procurement and SCM is the effective integration of procurement/SCM tasks with other organizational objectives. Supply chain tasks are balanced with other functional tasks to create a supply chain or procurement roadmap.[1] With this roadmap, strategic procurement and SCM is further defined

1. "Productivity Roadmap" is a purchasing tool used by the Ford Motor Company North American purchasing operations during the middle and late 1990s. The multidimensional supplier cost reduction plans identified as part of the productivity roadmap were used to determine purchasing strategies in delivering the identified cost reductions.

through the use of a business management system designed to pull all the elements together. Chapter 2 described hoshin planning/MBP as a business management system effective in integrating various strategic initiatives with individual performance tasks. The importance of using a business system to process the SCM efforts cannot be understated. Without this discipline, the strategies tend to become individual tasks appearing to have a flavor-of-the-month feel.

The success or effectiveness of strategic procurement is measured in broad supply chain and business measures. These measures differentiate strategic efforts from tactical performance. Tactical measures usually are only those centered on cost. Strategic performance objectives must extend to the business systems. In addition, all stakeholder needs must be included in supply chain plans and measures.

SCM AS A BUSINESS SYSTEM

It is uncommon for organizations to consider supply chain management as a business system. The common view is that SCM is a collection of efforts. Keeping with the strategic view of SCM it is critical to change this paradigm from a collection of efforts to a business system. In practice, this view is no different than the view of lean manufacturing as a business system.

The necessity of the system view is based on the fact that standalone SCM activities cannot be successful in the long term. Stand-alone activities are seen as events rather than as ongoing processes. Short-term events typically are not sustained and do not provide long-term direction or results. Strategic procurement must be viewed as an extension of a company's manufacturing strategy, marketing strategy, financial strategy, and customer strategy. A business systems approach shifts the view from events to processes, from limited to sustaining, and from short to long term. A holistic view must be taken of the procurement and SCM strategies, incorporating the various actions into a single initiative. The holistic approach is the development of the vision roadmap, which guides the process forward.

THE ABCs OF BUILDING A STRATEGIC SCM PLAN

When building the strategic procurement plan within a business system, the system must support flexibility. This is necessary because of the dynamics that are faced throughout a fiscal or planning year. Plans that are trapped by inflexible systems will not provide the responses necessary to maintain progress toward the long-term objectives. The following factors must be considered in the development of a lean supply chain strategic plan:

- *Procurement professionals must recognize the business situation present and plan for those conditions.* Too frequently procurement plans are developed independent of the environment in which they need to operate.
- *Long-term strategic is different than short-term strategic in scope and planning.* Inherent biases cause most businesspeople to associate strategic efforts with the long term. Equally important is to understand and embrace the concept of short-term strategic—that is, those efforts designed to be a building block for a complete SCM strategy. These efforts can be accomplished within a compressed period of time. (Much of the crisis plan efforts described in the prior chapters are based on short-term strategic concepts.)
- *Strategic procurement as part a business process depends on the use of a proven business system.* Entering into a strategic supply chain plan often represents a significant departure from the status quo. Attempting to simultaneously launch an SCM effort and develop an overall business system represents an unreasonable demand of business maturation.
- *Using recognized approaches versus homegrown methods provides ready-made tools to help drive processes.* Examples

of proven business processes include hoshin planning or balanced scorecard. These methods, and the success of their implementation, have been the subject of many professional and academic works that provide prepared tools to enable ease of implementation.

MARRYING THE PLAN TO THE BUSINESS SYSTEM

The successful incorporation of the strategic supply chain effort into the overall business environment depends upon the ability to link individual performance, organizational efforts, and management support of supply chain initiatives to the rest of the organization. To accomplish this task the development of the plan needs to consider, and the business system needs to demand, the interdependency of these objectives. Building upon the content of Chapter 2, the marriage of these two objectives can be accomplished through considering the following factors:

- *Plan SCM initiatives from corporate vision points or overarching objectives.* This means that all efforts in supply chain management (or any other functional department) are based on a set of universal expectations and performance efforts determined at the highest level in the organization.
- *Ensure coordination with other operational and functional objectives.* Often individual objectives come into direct conflict with other departments' efforts. The coordination of the SCM objectives with these other objectives ensures the future cross-organizational support often required for success as well as providing for a coordinated effort in achieving the overarching objectives.
- *Build the plan around stretch goals, but allow for successes during milestone reviews.* Because of the historic bias toward financial business plans, success isn't known until the completion of the plan. Although quarterly goals may be identified, milestone progress reviews outside of that are not widely used. Frequent reviews allow you to keep

the plan on track, but also to encourage the organization by recognizing the important progress that has been made toward the completion of a process item.

- *Ensure that measures address the business needs as defined by the business systems, broad-based financial and nonfinancial.* Typical SCM measures are financially driven. Chief among these measures is purchase price variance (PPV). While PPV is acceptable, the SCM measures need to broadly evaluate organizational contribution and effectiveness. PPV alone shifts actions to short-term financial measures only. Supply chain management should encompass supplier quality and development as well as the traditional purchasing, logistics, and distribution functions.

THE ELEMENTS OF A STANDARD ENVIRONMENT SCM PLAN

The elements that follow represent one of many outlines for a strategic SCM plan. The areas outlined represent the priority items that facilitate the most significant improvement, and, ultimately, contribution to the bottom line. The plan outlines six major areas of initiative within SCM. These areas represent the major elements of cost, quality, delivery, and support, as well as an internal focus on organizational skills and training.

- *Supply base management.* Broad supply base and commodity planning activities exemplified by:
  1. Identification and selection of fully capable suppliers to meet needs in product development (as appropriate), production and delivery support, and financial performance.
  2. Benchmarking and supplier consolidation activities to identify and select best–in-class suppliers.
- *Supplier quality.* Operational quality and development efforts with the following activities:
  1. Develop and implement integrated supplier quality expectations and measuring techniques.

2. Support benchmarking activities with focus on quality systems.
3. Establish supplier stratification methodology based on objective measures (e.g., PPM, PPAP, CAR, commercial and delivery).
4. Utilize quality planning tools to support operational requirements (QOS/TQM, APQP, 8D, etc.).

- *Cost management.* Developing costing approaches affecting longer term cost structure and next-generation pricing efforts, such as the following:
  1. Establish affordable cost target mechanism to achieve corporate profitability and customer target price objectives.
  2. Identify value management techniques to improve current product cost structures.
  3. Utilize process improvement techniques (e.g., kaizen, kaikaku, etc.) to assist supplier cost improvement.
- *Cost improvement.* Near-term and existing products cost improvement and price reduction actions, including:
  1. Focus near-term efforts on resourcing opportunities generated from benchmarking and consolidation activities.
  2. Focus long-term efforts on implementing partnership actions and multiyear productivity reductions.
  3. Develop annual commodity value management opportunity list and drive implementation.
  4. Utilize ACT on new part content.
- *Distribution, transportation, and logistics.* This includes material movement and handling improvement efforts such as:
  1. Develop visual factory scheme within warehouse and distribution operations to support improved order fill rate.
  2. Establish meaningful measurement method to monitor customer service and warehouse performance.
  3. Drive inbound transportation costs downward, targeting 10 percent cost improvement.

- *Organization.* Matching the performance expectations to necessary skills through evaluation and gap analysis with appropriate compensation and promotional opportunities, including:
  1. Evaluate classification and pay range structure for all materials positions.
  2. Establish specific position performance expectations and conduct gap analysis for all associates.
  3. Develop and implement a comprehensive training curriculum.

CASE STUDY 10.2

Questions

1. How would DSW determine if the SCM's contribution to the company's financial improvements was sufficient? What factors would or should DSW include in this evaluation?
2. What ways could the DSW SCM organization better coordinate its divisional efforts? How do these efforts vary depending on DSW's view on centralized or decentralized SCM?
3. Would DSW have any alternative in the way it manages inflationary effects on purchase content? How does the industry in which DSW operates affect the approach to inflationary effects?

Answers

1. DSW conducted an analysis of its total SCM costs including production parts cost; non-production parts cost; in-bound transportation costs (outbound is generally paid for by customer); supplier related inspection, detection, and containment cost for quality issues; and organizational expenses. This analysis examined a growth-adjusted total cost trend as compared to the growth-adjusted customer price reductions.

   Based on the material content contributed to the cost of goods, the expectation was for a 100 percent offset of SCM cost as a percentage of COGS. Year over year net dollar savings and givebacks were compared, with givebacks resulting in an approximate 3.5 percent revenue loss. With SCM cost approximately 65 percent of COGS, approximately 2.3 percent of the 3.5 percent needed to be offset by SCM savings. The historic savings of net 1.5 percent (3 percent savings—1 percent to 2 percent economics) falls nearly a full 1 percent short of the needed offset.

The translation of this offset level is that the requirements on DSW from its customers are more stringent than DSW to its suppliers. DSW's SCM organization achieves only 65 percent of the needed savings to maintain parity with its customer demands.

2. DSW had generally embraced a decentralized SCM structure. The effect of this was a lack of coordination in common commodities, suppliers, and pricing approaches. To counteract this effect, while maintaining divisional responsibility in SCM, DSW developed a hybrid organization in which common SCM services (such as freight, travel, etc.) were managed centrally; cross-divisional commodity teams were developed, with an assigned commodity champion managing the commodity and supplier strategy for the entire company, and with a centralized strategic procurement and supplier development group.

   Tying into the corporate overarching objectives as part of the MBP efforts, DSW developed a single set of departmental objectives consistent with its strategic plan efforts. The single set of objectives required a better coordination of all SCM efforts. Coupled with the hybrid structure, DSW was able to create a single face to its supply base, as well as internally.

3. DSW's primary product sales are in automotive and aerospace industries. Within the automotive sector (which represented 70+ percent of DSW sales) economic risk lies entirely with the supplier—no economic increases were passed through. In this vein, DSW adopted the same policy, contractually requiring the suppliers to manage all their own economic exposure. The effect of this was to increase the net savings level and increase the ability to plan for procurement performance throughout the fiscal year.

11

Supply Base Management

KNOWING WHAT YOU WANT

Among the many differences that U.S. automotive companies exhibit from Asian-based companies (in addition to the lean approach we discussed so far) is the time spent in preparation and planning prior to the attempted execution of individual tasks. In the traditional PDCA (plan-do-check-act) cycle approach to operational planning, the tendency in U.S. business is to spend little time on the "P" (plan) phase, and get to the "D" (do) phase as quickly as possible. The need to demonstrate progress is driven by the quarterly financial focus versus the long-term focus of many non-U.S. firms (particularly Japanese companies).

In lean supply chain management, the time spent in the planning phase must expand beyond the normal to provide the proper understanding of exactly what it is that needs to be accomplished. Without this planning effort, a significant amount of time is often spent on developing and implementing strategies to secure performance that your company many not even need. Integrating the supplier-based capabilities with the real company needs provides the greatest value from the supply chain.

The perceived need for various supplier capabilities is an example where planning can provide value. Many companies may believe that there is a need to develop "full service suppliers"[1] (FSS). The service provided by FSS suppliers (largely design and validation) includes a cost premium. However, the purchasing company often never utilizes these FSS services. Many labor-hours can be devoted to identifying and developing FSS organizations, validating the cost premiums for such suppliers, with the company never actually using or needing these capabilities.

This chapter focuses on planning the supply base strategy and knowing exactly what is required from those suppliers.

IMPLEMENTING SUPPLY BASE MANAGEMENT

Just as the planning activities in the crisis plan followed a specific structure, so too does the planning in the standard environment. To ensure that the plan is consistent with and in support of the overarching corporate objectives, the standard plan specifically addresses the strategic initiative as well as the implementation plan for each of the plan's elements. From these plan definitions, the individual tools for delivering the performance are created and utilized. The implementation plan and the associated tools are where the "rubber hits the road" in translating plans to action.

---

1. "Full service supplier" is a term used by Ford Motor Company in defining suppliers with the capabilities to develop subsystem design parameters; the ability to integrate and manage lower tier suppliers; and, generally the ability to absorb a significant portion of the design, development, testing, and prove out of products which had previously been done by Ford. In classifying suppliers as "FSS" suppliers, there was an increased level of capabilities necessary from the normal suppliers, as well as an expanded evaluation and certification procedure.

CASE STUDY 11.1

DWS recognized the need to develop a central organization that was responsible for the development of a single supply base strategy. This strategy and supply base would be designed to support the various operating divisions with a common supplier quality system and development effort. The centralized team would also be responsible for the roll-up of total commodity savings, including the negotiations of multi-year sourcing and pricing agreements.

To secure the broadest base of support of the selected supply base, the SCM organization recruited the support and participation of other functional department personnel. The other participants were responsible for helping to define the supply base needs and supplier qualifications.

Questions

1. Why would it be necessary to enlist the support of other organizations to accomplish tasks that would clearly be SCM responsibilities? What is the risk in getting (or not getting) this support?
2. How would DSW's SCM organization accurately determine the needs of the company with respect to supplier capabilities? How would these capabilities be valued?
3. Is there a method by which DSW could be sure to include a supply base evaluation beyond the typical view of production suppliers only? Why is this important and how do you quantify the impact?

Strategic Initiative

The strategic initiative should be to provide a competitive advantage to company performance by developing a self-sufficient supply base capable of providing world class designs, products, quality, and customer support. Through benchmarking of supplier capabilities, supply consolidation and base reduction will allow for improved customer of choice service and response. The services should specifically include the following:

- Engineering capabilities able to provide component design and product development as required by commodity demands.
- Value chain management capabilities capable of delivering price improvement and cost containment resulting in annual purchase order price reductions.
- Organizational and managerial flexibility to respond to changes in cost control and price improvement, increasing quality requirements, and technology and design advancement.

Implementation Plan

The plan outlines a supply base benchmarking and consolidation strategy aimed at optimizing the supply base to meet the competitive cost needs, design requirements, quality expectations, and customer service support. To this end, a structured approach includes:

- *A commodity cycle plan.* This is a planning tool detailing purchase information, specifically forecasting future year purchases, pricing levels, and total commodity acquisition.
- *Commodity benchmarking techniques.* The development of an approach and tools for evaluating and comparing supplier capabilities.
- *Benchmarking and comparative analysis.* This is a cross-functional capabilities assessment and force ranking of commodity suppliers. This activity drives stratification, consolidation, and future sourcing patterns.

- *Supply base selection and redefinition.* This uses the data from the benchmarking efforts and establishes a specific methodology for determining retained and new suppliers into the commodity and supply base.
- *Consolidation and cost savings opportunities.* This involves quantifying and planning cost improvement roadmaps for individual suppliers and commodities.
- *Execution of long-term agreements.* This involves establishing pro forma contract requirements detailing economic curtailment and price improvement terms covering multi-year sourcing.
- *Definition of commercial and quality expectations.* This involves establishing ongoing supplier performance measures designed to drive supply base stratification and sourcing decisions.
- *Ongoing supply base maintenance.* This involves providing methodologies of entry into and elimination from the supply base, using industry standards for quality and operating systems.

COMMODITY CYCLE PLANNING

Data acquisition and analysis is key in planning any effort. The lean SCM work derived from the standard environment is based upon the future profile of the aggregated product and service purchases. Traditionally, historic data is used in determining supply base commercial performance and expectations. Unfortunately, this data can be viewed as interesting, but unimportant. The information is interesting in that it provides a glimpse of past performance, but is unimportant in that it provides little vision of the future requirements.

A commodity cycle plan (CCP) is a commodity level detailed view of aggregated buy, both current and future forecast. The importance of this information is that it provides a basis upon which the SCM organization can build an expectation of improved financial performance through buy growth; provides the basis on which point leverage[2] negotiation opportunities can be defined and capitalized on; and provides economic impact forecasts, which can be used in the financial planning and performance process.

Figure 11.1 is a simplified example of a CCP. The primary elements of the CCP are:

- Supplier level summaries.
- Individual program (or material type if bulk or commodity materials) listing.
- Purchase content per vehicle or program (a roll-up of all parts on specific platform).
- Annual extended cost per program per year for four-year planning horizon.
- Total purchases per year per supplier.
- Aggregate purchases for all suppliers within the commodity for each year in the planning horizon.

The tool provides a snapshot view of the coming sourcing pattern, and helps to identify additional sourcing opportunities available in consolidation efforts. Not identified in the example, but of tremendous benefit, is the identification of future unsourced parts. Through the use of cost estimates, the unsourced parts and programs provide for negotiation planning well in advance of sourcing actions, furthering the point leverage approach.

---

2. Point leverage is a technique used to create buy leverage in environments in which "natural" leverage does not exist. The natural leverage is absent primarily due to the lack of significant size in transaction quantities. The point leverage approach creates for a short time a similar size component allowing a negotiating advantage.

Commodity 1
Commodity Cycle Plan

Supplier 1	$ / Vehicle	2003	2004	2005	2006
Prog 1	$36.00	$4,320,000	$3,420,000	$3,420,000	$3,456,000
Prog 2	$36.00	$360,000	$720,000	$900,000	$972,000
Total:		$4,680,000	$4,140,000	$4,320,000	$4,428,000
Supplier 2	**$ / Vehicle**	**2003**	**2004**	**2005**	**2006**
Prog 3	$22.40	$5,712,000	$2,228,800	$0	$0
Prog 4	$43.00	$13,717,000	$12,857,000	$0	$0
Prog 10	$36.25	$0	$0	$3,625,000	$9,062,500
Prog 5	$20.80	$2,294,822	$0	$0	$0
Total:		$21,723,822	$15,085,800	$3,625,000	$9,062,500
Supplier 3	**$ / Vehicle**	**2003**	**2004**	**2005**	**2006**
Prog 4	$31.20			$9,984,000	$9,984,000
Prog 1	$35.20	$8,448,000	$6,687,994	$6,687,997	$6,758,400
Prog 2	$35.20	$704,000	$1,408,000	$1,760,000	$1,900,800
Prog 6	$37.60		$5,136,912	$10,422,720	$10,571,616
Total:		$9,152,000	$13,232,906	$28,854,717	$29,214,816
Supplier 4	**$ / Vehicle**	**2003**	**2004**	**2005**	**2006**
Prog 7	$29.00		$1,983,600	$3,958,500	$3,970,100
Prog 8	$39.40	$295,500	$689,500	$689,500	$689,500
Prog 9					
Total:		$295,500	$2,673,100	$4,648,000	$4,659,600
Grand Total:		**$35,851,322**	**$35,131,806**	**$41,447,717**	**$47,364,916**

Figure 11.1 Commodity Cycle Plan

COMMODITY PRO FORMA

Directly tied to the future forecast data of the commodity cycle plan is an overview of commodity performance. The commodity pro forma provides a complete commodity financial summary, including annual buy data, forecasted savings per year attributed to long-term agreements and consolidation efforts, as well as a summary of targeted suppliers within the supply base and the effect of inflationary offsets. The roll-up of the individual commodity pro formas provides a total acquisition savings summary that can be used as the basis for corporate financial planning. From the reported levels, the gap from the required annual performance to the rolled up total provides the specific levels that need to be bridged. Figure 11.2 shows a completed commodity pro forma. The highlighted fields represent the areas requiring buyer intervention and completion, while the balance of the document is programmed to be auto-calculated.

This planning document demonstrates the increasing level of savings achieved each year through increased long-term contract coverage, savings obtained in consolidation driven by decreasing the supply base, and incremental offsets to inflationary factors. The cap listed in the absorbed economics portion represents the high end of the inflationary move that the suppliers are contractually bound to accept. Driving the programming of this document is a fairly in-depth level of inflationary forecasts for material, labor, and overhead factors.

COMMODITY SUPPLIER BENCHMARKING

Benchmarking techniques usually imply measuring your own processes against others to assess performance, and perhaps identifying best practices (assuming the participants have best practices in place). Unfortunately for the buying organizations, most suppliers have not participated in a full system benchmarking activity and are unable to objectively provide compar-

Commodity 2

Total current sources:	6				
Target # of sources:	4				
		2003	**2004**	**2005**	**2006**
# Suppliers		6	5	5	4
LTA Coverage		25%	25%	75%	95%
Annual Buy		$11,660,397	$12,321,414	$14,060,439	$16,806,418
Forcasted Economic Exposure (FY03-06)					
Material:		$129,512	$103,820	$118,473	$141,611
Labor:		$48,974	$45,836	$52,305	$62,520
Overhead:		$161,730	$170,898	$195,018	$233,105
Total economic exposure		$340,215	$320,554	$365,796	$437,236
Forcasted annual buy + exposure		$12,000,612	$12,641,967	$14,426,235	$17,243,654

Planned Cost Savings and Avoidance

Savings:					
Net productivity	4.5%	$131,179	$138,616	$474,540	$718,474
Resourcing / negotiate	2.5%	$72,877	$77,009	$263,633	$399,152
Total savings		$204,057	$215,625	$738,173	$1,117,627
Avoidances:					
Material	5% cap	$32,378	$25,955	$88,855	$134,530
Labor		$48,974	$45,836	$52,305	$62,520
Overhead		$161,730	$170,898	$195,018	$233,105
Total avoidances		243,081	$242,689	$336,178	$430,155
Total savings and avoidances		$447,138	$458,313	$1,074,351	$1,547,782
Net Fiscal Year Impact		$(106,923)	$(137,760)	$(708,555)	$(1,110,546)

Figure 11.2 Commodity Pro Forma

ison to competitors. Commodity benchmarking serves to provide this service for the suppliers. Of consideration in developing a benchmarking activity is the belief that institutional quality certifications such as ISO9000, QS9000, etc., do not provide for a certainty of capability, but simply adherence to internal work instruction procedures. Benchmarking, by contrast, evaluates and ranks various determinants of capabilities in relation to an expected standard as well as in contrast to others evaluated.

Figure 11.3 provides a workflow analysis of a benchmarking process. The initial steps rely on the information in the CCP in determining the needed number of suppliers based on annual expenditures as well as commodity complexity. It is from this basis that the analysis selects the supplier needed. In addition, the effort relies on a cross-functional team for determining the supplier base as to create "our suppliers" vs. "purchasing's suppliers".

Upon the completion of the benchmarking evaluations, a force ranking is completed to select the targeted number of suppliers. These suppliers are debriefed with respect to the observed results, and are provided anonymous comparisons to others that have been reviewed to provide benchmarking data that is otherwise unobtainable. It is on the results of the benchmarking visits and observations that ongoing improvement efforts are based. Suppliers falling short of the benchmark force ranking level are debriefed and details are given as to the reason for their elimination from the supply base.

During the debrief process the opportunity for incremental business through consolidation and open sourcing is utilized to secure agreement to specific terms of business, including agreement to annual price improvements, management and absorption of inflationary economics, and adherence to other commercial and quality requirements. This point of negotiation is where the maximum leverage exists, and it should be wisely utilized in securing the most favorable commercial agreements.

Supplier benchmarking is not an ongoing process, but a point process that is used on an infrequent basis. Conducting such a

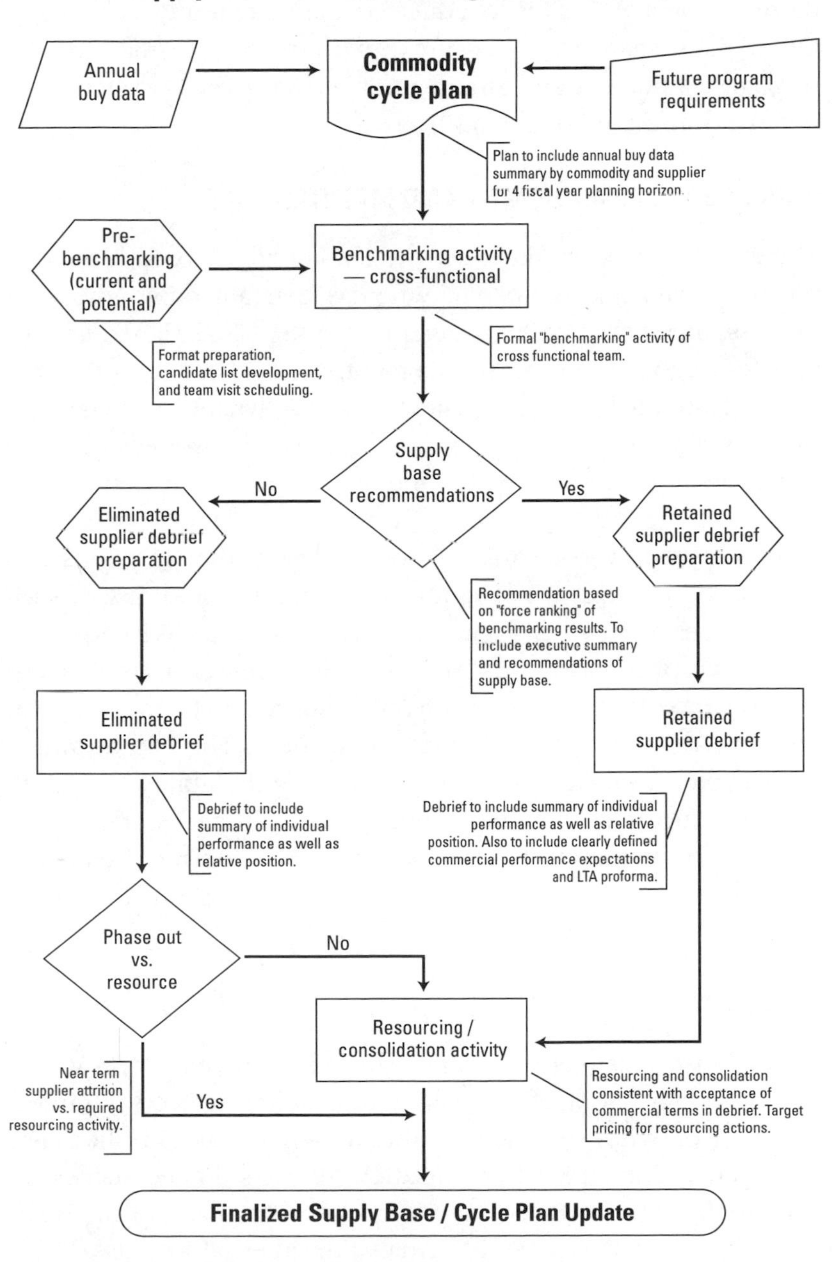

Figure 11.3 Benchmarking and Consolidation

process is typically beneficial only every four to five years, or if there is a major shift in product or manufacturing technology. Other maintenance systems are put into place to manage the ongoing evaluation and stratification efforts. These systems are reviewed in the following section.

SUPPLY BASE DEVELOPMENT AND MAINTENANCE

The supplier benchmarking activity leads into a closed loop supply base management system. Whereas benchmarking is a point process, the supply base management system is designed to provide for ongoing supplier management. Figure 11.4 shows the way in which supply base management takes on dynamic management by providing for entry assessments, performance measures and stratification, elimination plans, and annual strategy reviews.

Dynamic supply base management means that methods are established to expand and contract the number and mix of suppliers in response to changing product and business needs. The use of supplier scorecards or other measures ensures that the performance of existing suppliers is sufficient to meeting the growing and changing demands of business. The use of industry accepted evaluation processes provides the ability to qualify and introduce new suppliers where and when necessary (Figure 11.4 reflects automotive standards from SQ9000 requirements). The annual supply strategy reviews puts these actions into place when defining future sourcing strategies.

SUMMARY

Supply base management is the backbone process upon which other strategic SCM efforts can build. Without a clear understanding of who, how many, and in what way suppliers are managed within an SCM organization, there is limited success in structurally achieving sustained improvement in any of the quality, cost, and delivery metrics. Analyzing internal buy data, supplier performance, and methods of evaluation provides a clear basis with which to move forward.

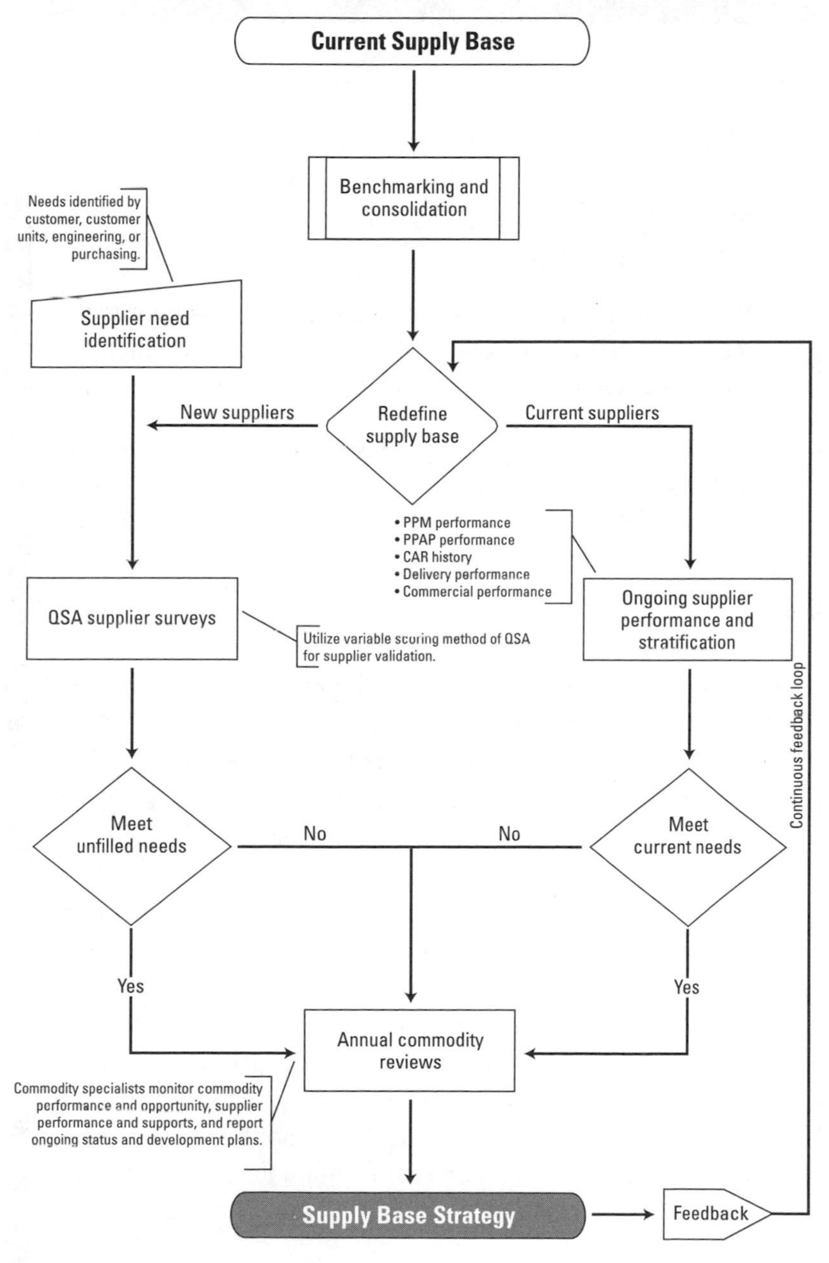

Figure 11.4 Supply Base Development

CASE STUDY 11.2

Questions:

1. Why would it be necessary to enlist the support of other organizations to accomplish tasks that would clearly be SCM responsibilities? What is the risk in getting (or not getting) this support?
2. How would DSW's SCM organization accurately determine the needs of the company with respect to supplier capabilities? How would these capabilities be valued?
3. Is there a method by which DSW could be sure to include a supply base evaluation beyond the typical view of production suppliers only? Why is this important and how do you quantify the impact?

Answers

1. Historically, DSW was victim to finger-pointing when suppliers failed to perform in either program launch or production support. Functional groups within the organization would blame the supplier selected by purchasing, or selected by engineering, or someone else for the problems that were being experienced. The perception was that if "they" (i.e., the functional groups) had had the chance to provide input into sourcing or make the decision, these issues would not have occurred.

   Including the major functional areas in the benchmarking and selection process gave each group input into which supplier made up the new supply base. Because of this, while any specific individual may not have selected a specific supplier, someone representing their interests and part of their organization did participate. The supply base now becomes "our suppliers" versus anything else. The risk of not including these other functions is not only in a lack of acceptance, but may actually result in creating failure of performance.

2. The preparation phase or pre-benchmarking activity brought an analysis of the historic issue in part and supplier performance. In addition, an assessment was completed of the anticipated technology and usage shifts for future commodity applications. It was on the basis of this information that the scope of required supplier capabilities was determined. In some cases design capabilities were required of the suppliers, and in other commodities they were not required.

   The capabilities were valued in a total cost of acquisition model, contrasting internal costs with procured costs. Internal profitability rates were set for all processes, and through a classic make-buy analysis were evaluated for each acquisition plan. Affordable cost target methods were implemented to ensure cost creep did not occur.

3. DSW expanded its view of SCM to encompass all elements of the value chain. By changing its view, all acquired goods and services affecting product value, whether production or not, was subject to the same scrutiny and strategic initiatives. The importance of this scrutiny lies in the fact that most organizations will have an incremental cost base of 25 to 35 percent above the production cost level. Savings achieved from this base may actually exceed production savings due to the newness of evaluation—the low hanging fruit hasn't been harvested yet.

12

Supplier Quality and Development

QUALITY VERSUS DEVELOPMENT

Organizations that embrace supplier quality responsibilities as part of SCM generally approach the issue with a focus on quality resolution. Simply fixing supplier related quality issues to provide immediate containment in support of operational concerns usually does not provide systemic resolution to the underlying cause of these problems. Because of this dichotomy of effort to resolution, distinguishing between supplier quality and supplier development is an important issue.

Supplier quality is the organizational effort required to contain supplier problems, working toward a permanent corrective action. The problem resolution approach in a supplier quality organization is generally reactive in nature, responding to situations that have already occurred. Significant labor hours are spent in containment and detection of quality issues measured and reported typically in parts per million (PPM) defect levels. By contrast, little time is spent on prevention, and assistance to suppliers not hitting the radar screen is often nonexistent.

Supplier development includes a longer-horizon view of supplier support. The developmental activities are geared toward aiding in the construction of robust manufacturing and quality systems to eliminate the potential for product failures. Development efforts work almost entirely on the prevention of quality problems, seeking to institutionalize the ability to detect and contain random reject occurrences. Allocation of supplier support time is based upon the output of commodity and supplier analysis, performance stratification, and commodity team determination.

SUPPLIER QUALITY AND SUPPLIER DEVELOPMENT PLAN

Strategic initiative

The strategic initiative here is to develop a self-contained supplier quality assurance (SQA) department within the corporate materials function. The strategic focus of this activity is to develop best-in-class supplier quality expectations and performance measuring methodologies. Through these efforts supplier manufacturing quality capabilities will be driven through QS9000 requirements, standardization of performance to AIAG methods and standards, and OEM quality expectations.

Implementation Plan

The implementation plan starts with the application of defined quality metrics (PPM, PPAP, DCAR, delivery, commercial, etc.) to stratify the supply base based on ongoing performance. The QS9000 QSA can be used as a supplier audit methodology to verify supplier capability and improvement gains.

Departmental structure reflects the varying needs for supplier quality support. Tactical (daily operational) support monitors and corrects immediate production support issues. PPAP submission, DCAR resolution, and postreadiness review launch support is maintained within the operation facilities by supplier

CASE STUDY 12.1

Organizationally, DSW's supplier quality staff reported through the purchasing organization with a quality engineer reporting directly to a commodity buyer. The plant level activities such as part inspection and approval were independent from the on-site supplier containment efforts. Each of the operating units individually determined their desire for and need of supplier quality support.

While determining the integrated SCM strategy, DSW began to consider the efforts that would be required to represent quality functional objectives, along with post-benchmarking efforts required to perpetuate a greatly enhanced supply base.

Questions

1. Is the organizational structure supporting supplier quality at DSW sufficient to assist the SCM organization in moving its supply base forward? If not, what alternative exists to do this?
2. How are development activities accomplished within organizations structured as DSW is structured? Under this scenario, how is the division of supplier improvement tasks accomplished?
3. What should be the ongoing role of supplier quality or supplier development in DSW?

quality engineers (SQE) and supplier quality technicians (SQT). Strategic development support is geared toward systemic supplier quality problem resolution. Through the application of quality planning tools (e.g., APQP, QFD, 8D, etc.), and through the application of ongoing performance indicators, strategic supplier development engineers serve as technical consultants to work with and resolve reoccurring supplier quality issues.

SUPPLIER QUALITY DEVELOPMENT STRUCTURE

Neither supplier quality nor supplier development is generally considered part of supply chain management. Part of the issue is the definition of supply chain management as discussed in Chapter 1, in which supply chain management is generally considered material movement. The more likely reason is that quality is generally considered an operational responsibility and not a supply chain element. Unfortunately, in the hierarchy of redress for quality concerns, supplier issues are treated like the "ugly redheaded stepchild" by the quality organization. Customer issues receive highest priority. Internal quality issues come second, with supplier issues a distant third. The third place attention only comes when resources may be available.

Organizational options geared toward supporting both tactical and developmental responsibilities are normally constrained by limited resources. Most companies cannot increase staffing levels to accommodate developmental efforts. Figure 12.1 provides an example of using limited resources in multiple roles to create the skill and knowledge base capable of providing the developmental support. This organizational option clearly delineates between tactical and developmental responsibilities. The purpose of this differentiation is to ensure that the limited developmental resources are not diverted into daily problem-solving activities.

IMPROVING SUPPLIER PERFORMANCE

In working toward achieving long-lasting development efforts, the SCM development team must focus on three fundamental areas: performance stratification of the supply base, development of specific corrective actions, and the use of process specialists to

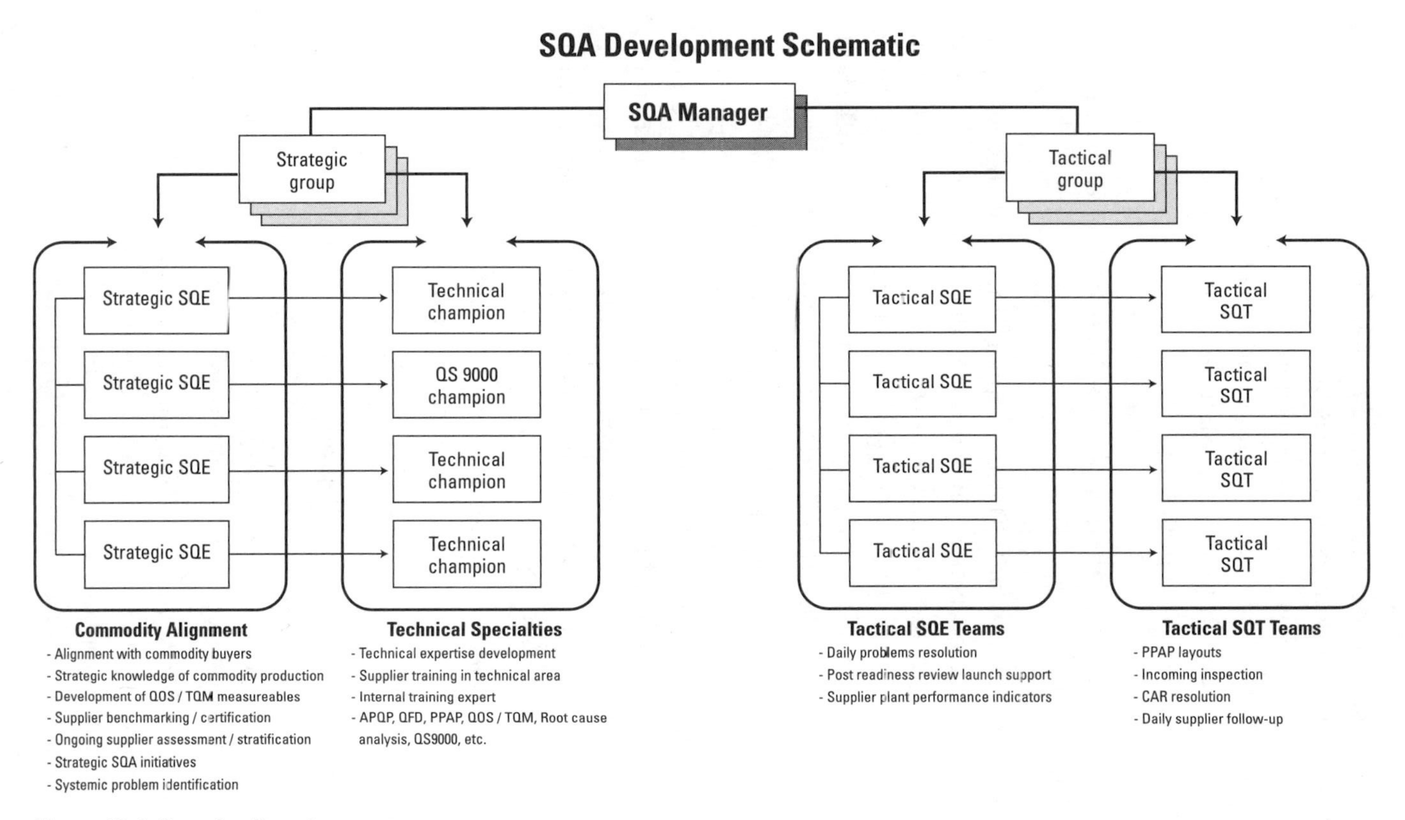

Figure 12.1 Supplier Development

attack systemic quality issues. In each commodity, supplier development identifies and measures performance characteristics on which development focus and sourcing preference will be based. The data accumulation and resulting ranks provide objective sourcing plans, consistent with industry requirements (such as approved supplier lists).

The stratification of the supply base can be based on the following criteria:

- *Preferred partner.* These suppliers meet the highest performance measures. They achieve all commercial and quality supplier requirements as well as all program development milestones and launch requirements. These suppliers can generally be considered self–sufficient, requiring little or no specific development efforts.
- *Associate partner.* These suppliers have generally consistent quality practices and exhibit predictable product, delivery, and support performance. Occasional quality problems result in lowered stratification scores, requiring a greater level of development support. It is generally this classification toward which the majority of development efforts are geared.
- *Probationary partner.* This stratification level indicates a supplier with obvious deficit performance, but that has been identified as necessary for the supply bases. Suppliers under this classification retain existing business but are ineligible to be considered for additional business. Supplier quality activities are present in this level over development efforts. The focus on containment and specific problem resolution occupies the improvement efforts.
- *Transition supplier.* Transition suppliers are those with deficit performance, with no development plans in place. These suppliers will be phased out either through active resourcing or attrition of existing parts.

The second primary area of focus is the development of specific corrective action strategies for each category of stratification defined in the preceding list. This effort balances the tactical quality effort and resources with the development effort and resources, creating a targeted focus versus a random approach to effort allocation.

The third area in supply base development is the use of supplier quality engineers and supplier development engineers as process specialists to attack and correct systemic quality issues. By leveraging resources, the assignment of quality or development champions provides significant improvements across the entire supply base.

CUSTOMER/SUPPLIER RELATIONSHIPS

Among the most difficult issues to resolve in supplier quality and development is the definition of the relationship between the customer and supplier. The naming convention of the stratification levels is designed to convey the intent behind each of the levels. At those levels in which support activities are to be provided, the stratification identifies the suppliers as partners. While this is an overused and seldom followed term, partners imply a cooperative effort in obtaining performance improvements.

Depending on the size and complexity of the customer, direction and communication to the supplier can often provide mixed messages concerning the expected performance and nature of the relationship. There are a number of simple relationship steps that can be taken to facilitate improved communication and relationship between supplier and customer. Among those are:

- Identify a supplier quality assurance commodity specialist to facilitate single point quality contact (i.e., to be a liaison between the customer and supplier).

- Improve the consistency of direction to the supplier.
- Use published industry quality standards as the basis for supplier quality standards.
- Develop and implement a supplier recognition program for key measurables.
- Drive PPAP (production parts approval process) to level I and IV self-certification.

Each of these points creates a simple means to improve communication and recognition of supplier performance.

CASE STUDY 12.2

Questions

1. Is the organizational structure supporting supplier quality at DSW sufficient to assist the SCM organization in moving its supply base forward? If not, what alternative exists to do this?
2. How are development activities accomplished within organizations structured as DSW is structured? Under this scenario, how is the division of supplier improvement tasks accomplished?
3. What should be the ongoing role of supplier quality or supplier development in DSW?

Answers

1. While an integrated SCM approach led by a commodity buyer may have benefit, this organization would not provide the quality functional leadership necessary to ensure the knowledge base required. DSW incorporated a supplier development director as a direct report to the VP of

SCM, creating a peer relationship with purchasing and distribution/logistics. The effect of this move was to create matrixed partners assigned by the commodity group and strategic or tactical support.

2. Generally, supplier development activities are not accomplished within organizations like DSW's initial structure. There really is no division of labor, as the entire focus is on reactive supplier quality versus long-term supplier development.

3. The ongoing role of supplier quality and development should be one in which resources are utilized in support of the overall SCM initiative, and by association with the corporate overarching objectives. While quality progress is rarely translated in profit impact, DSW chose to quantify the improvement to demonstrate the contribution to the company's bottom line.

13

Cost Management and Control

COST MANAGEMENT VERSUS CONTROL

The procurement arm of SCM is traditionally the part of the organization responsible for delivering cost improvement in SCM. Historically this activity has come full circle from annual open quoting, to long-term contracts with built-in reductions, back to open quoting via electronic auction sites. While the technology of achieving this type of savings has progressed, the underlying philosophy has not. This simple process relies almost entirely on market forces, treats all suppliers the same regardless of performance or capability, and takes very little thought or creativity in deployment. This approach isn't entirely bad, and may be effectively applied in pure commodity market purchases. The application isn't nearly as simple with custom and engineered products. Often, industry quality standards limit the universe of suppliers able to quote, as in the case of automotive where QS9000 requires an approved supplier list on which sourcing must be based. Because of this, the open quote approach fails either because of the limited participants or because of the inclusion of nonapproved suppliers for the sole purpose of whipsawing price.

The acceptance of open quoting is driven by its simplicity, but also by the view of responsibility regarding cost improvement. Where cost reduction is seen solely as a purchasing issue, all other SCM efforts disconnect from the cost objective. Expanding the view of cost from price to complete value chain—or total cost of acquisition (TCA) or total cost of ownership (TCO)—requires a broader and more inclusive approach to cost management. It is with this broader view that the various approaches can be separated into cost management and cost control. Simply stated, cost management includes those activities that affect the basic cost structure of a product. Cost control includes those activities that result in the reduction of the cost or price of existing products. These can be seen as having long- and short-term effects. Using analogies from our lean discussion, cost management equals kaizen, whereas cost control equals kaikaku.

STRATEGIC COST MANAGEMENT AND CONTROL

The business plan initiative for cost management and cost control encompasses a variety of elements. The initative is a straightforward articulation of the desired effort, but the implementation plan needs to take on individual subelements to deliver the objective results. In the implementation profile there are five major subsets: 1) immediate cost control initiatives (which is the most closely tied to short term profit improvement); 2) cost management initiatives; 3) cost target setting process creation (which will be used as a subset of cost management); 4) value management initiatives; and 5) process improvements. It is the combined use of these five elements that affect the multiple functional areas with which institutionalized cost reductions can be achieved in an ongoing fashion.

Strategic Initiative

The strategic initiative here is to develop cost management practices that institutionalize cost reduction and quality improvement

CASE STUDY 13.1

The supply chain management organization within DSW had structured its organization to support the various internal customer demands related to supply availability, delivery, quality, and price. In these areas substantive improvement had been achieved, with increasing levels in the rate of improvement. With the development of the objectives of the organization, the size and deployment of the personnel resources had increased.

With the new scope of responsibility, the financial contribution that the SCM organization was making also increased. However, while there was an increase in the procurement contributions, there was not a clear understanding of the impact, if any, that other parts of the SCM organization were making toward cost improvement. Because of this the organization started to come under fire from other departments.

Questions

1. In what ways could the supply chain organization contribute to the cost management and cost improvement of the company?
2. Why was the SCM group unable to articulate the full level of savings contribution that was being made? What could be done differently to better articulate the full scope of savings?
3. DSW's VP of Supply Chain Management was concerned about the overemphasis on the financial impact of the SCM contributions. What can be done to alleviate these concerns?

throughout the supply base. The implementation and execution of these initiatives is completed through a cooperative effort with the supply base, to ensure equity and participation.

Implementation Plan

The following list examines the elements of an effective cost management and cost control implementation plan:

- *Cost control and improvement.* This includes:
  1. Specific and precise identification of increasing annual price improvement and cost reduction tasks consistent with industry and commodity conditions (i.e., individualized commodity strategies).
  2, Kaikaku-focused (near-term) efforts primarily driven from resourcing opportunities generated as outcomes of benchmarking and consolidation activities.
  3. Kaizen-focused (longer-term) efforts on implementing collaborative supplier improvement actions and multi-year sourcing agreements (including quality, cost, and delivery improvement requirements).
  4. Annual value chain analysis identifying annual commodity improvement with achievable implementation.
- *Cost management.* This element involves:
  1. Using affordable cost target (ACT) based sourcing processes. The ACT sourcing methodology is based upon achieving program-specific corporate profitability objectives and meeting customer program-level target price requirements.
  2. Launching a supplier development process deploying kaizen- and kaikaku-based techniques to assist suppliers' ability to deliver immediate and sustained cost improvement.
- *Cost target setting.* This involves:
  1. Creating target-setting methodologies for use in source selection efforts (cost management initiative).

   2. Creating a supplier cost database (supply data warehouse) to identify and record surrogate target prices and target conformance success to enable financial goal setting for future programs.
   3. Through design for assembly/design for manufacturing (DFA/DFM) modeling, deploying a process to capture design and production cost-reduction opportunities.
   4. In conjunction with target setting methods, using a multidimensional logic-based detail quote analysis and pricing techniques for final source selection.
- *Value management.* This involves:
   1. Evaluating full supply value stream cost elements to identify supply chain savings opportunities.
   2. Using VA/VE workshops to facilitate identification of design-based savings, and using data to enable opportunity forecasting in like-product platforms.
   3. Institutionalizing value management data retention to a linkage methodology to retain lessons learned for next-generation product design.
   4. Incorporating supplier value management goals into commercial expectations and supplier performance monitoring.
- *Supply chain process improvement.* This involves:
   1. Introducing process improvement techniques (kaizen/kaikaku) to the supply base, providing process facilitation throughout the supply and value chain.
   2. Creating an institutionalized process improvement focus through the incorporation of cost control methods into the MBP system.
   3. Modeling all supply base process improvement initiatives to an internal lean methodology standard ensuring coordination in lean efforts.

Each of these elements is examined in more detail in the following sections.

1. COST CONTROL AND IMPROVEMENT

Annual Cost Reductions

In many industries cost control (meaning regularly occurring and planned cost reductions) is achieved by the rapid development of technology. This is especially true in computer, telecommunications, and other technology industries. Unfortunately not all industries share a similar fortune, with many fighting to achieve cost and price improvements over time. Standard environment supply chain plans need to include an element of price improvement by necessity. Although many industries do not experience the effects of technology driven savings, the marketplace in which products are sold continues to face downward price pressure driven either from consumer demands or from products imported from lower-cost global regions.

Annualized price reductions have historically been targeted in a random fashion. The method of determining what the required level of cost improvement should be in total, by commodity or by supplier, has often been one of guessing, hope, and prayer. There generally is little business logic behind these levels, although there are some very simple ways in which to put sense behind the demands. Figure 13.1 demonstrates one such approach. This tool incorporates enterprise-wide cost reduction needs, general market conditions, and commodity specific factors to derive a specific supplier level cost improvement target. In addition to these market factors driving price reduction, this format also includes consideration of previously achieved reductions. The combination of these elements provides a logical basis for supplier- and commodity-specific cost or price reductions.

Kaikaku: Benchmarking and Consolidation

In the standard environment, short-term cost savings can be achieved through managing market forces as defined in the previous paragraphs or through active intervention. Like the

Supplier PPV Target Establishment Form

Commodity ______________________________

Buyer ______________________ Supplier ______________________

I. Corporate Objective (PPV) ________%

II. Commodity Objective

A. Market condition influences

1. Competitive situation
   - a) Many competitors -______%
   - b) Few competitors N/C_____
   - c) No competitors +______%
2. Raw material pricing
   - a) Forecasted decrease -______%
   - b) Forecasted/contract hold N/C_____
   - c) Forecasted increase +______%
3. Currency/exchange rate
   - a) Forecasted decrease -______%
   - b) Forecasted/contract hold N/C_____
   - c) Forecasted increase +______%
4. Technology trends
   - a) Many technology advances -______%
   - b) Few/no technology advances N/C____%
5. Business levels/opportunities
   - a) Increasing business -______%
   - b) Stable business N/C_____
   - c) Decreasing business +______%
6. Other ____________ +/-______%

Commodity Total ________%

III. Supplier Objective

A. Contractural requirements -______%

B. VA/VE opportunities

1. Many opportunities -______%
2. Few opportunities N/C_____

C. Market position influences

1. Levels of business
   - a) $\geq$ 10% -______%
   - b) < 10% N/C_____
2. Levels of business in industry
   - a) $\geq$ 50% -______%
   - b) < 50% N/C_____
3. Consolidation opportunities
   - a) Many opportunities -______%
   - b) Few/no opportunities N/C_____
4. Other ____________ +/-______%

Supplier Total ________%

IV. Overall Target

Corporate Objective ________%
Commodity Objective ________%
Supplier Objective ________%
Total ________%

Figure 13.1 PPV Target Form

establishment of the annualized price improvement, these interventions can often lack the objective bases for decisionmaking. Consolidation in supply chain management occurs in nearly every industry, usually without reason. Capabilities benchmarking, like that detailed in Chapter 11 and shown in Figure 11.3 defines a process that uses comparative data and support tools to target specific levels of supply base structure. From these specific consolidation plans, a targeted savings level can be pursued for incorporation into a near-term savings initiative.

As discussed previously, kaikaku actions focus on structured radical change for the purpose of achieving improvement in the short term. Benchmarking and consolidation fit precisely with this definition. Figure 13.2 shows typical timing of implementing a benchmarking process. In this process, evaluation, consolidation planning, cost improvement, and beginning steps of actual consolidation occur for major commodity groupings within 12 months. Concurrent commodity reviews can occur based on the resources available.

Kaizen Actions: Long Term Savings and Quality Agreements

Part of the cost control actions resulting from benchmarking and consolidation includes the ability to achieve multiyear agreements outlining improvements in price, quality, delivery, and other commercial terms. The resourcing opportunities identified as part of the consolidation actions, along with a narrower supply base, create leveraged ongoing sourcing opportunities and an environment in which the required improvements can be captured. This redefining of the commercial environment provides the bridge between shorter-term cost improvement and longer-term cost management. By building in a known savings threshold, the SCM organization is able to provide definitive information to the annual financial plan on which profit forecasts can be based.

Task name	Duration
Commodity Cycle Plan	**85 days**
Strategic purchasing mtg	1 day
Distribution of 5-year plans	31 days
Compile data	35 days
Strategic downoad	1 day
Compile future data	16 days
CCP rollout meeting	1 day
Benchmarking Team	**47 days**
Executive team charter	1 day
CU/AE appointees	46 days
Survey development	24 days
Survey review and approval	1 day
Commodity Summary	**271 days**
Schedule benchmarking visits	10 days
Benchmarking visits	99 days
Executive summary	10 days
Supply base recommendation	1 day
Prepare debrief packages	5 days
Supplier debriefs	15 days
Consolidation plan	15 days
Contract negotiation	131 days

Figure 13.2 Benchmarking Timing

Figure 13.3 shows the importance of secured multiyear price reduction agreements on net cost impact. This form shows the increase in contract coverage (as a percentage of purchase price) resulting in an average 3.5 percent per year price reduction. Also, the contracts typically require full supplier responsibility of economic movements[1] further contributing to the net savings amount. Finally, the reduction in the number of suppliers in the base drives increases in annual expenditures under contract, as well as expenditures available for consolidation and resourcing savings. Like the example in the crisis environment, target prices used during the price benchmarking allow for incremental savings. Figure 13.3 shows an average 3 percent saving on resourcing efforts.

2. COST MANAGEMENT

Cost management differs greatly from cost control in that cost management focuses on the long-term institutionalization of supply chain business practices aimed at achieving and maintaining cost savings trends. The efforts undertaken here represent fundamental business practices versus individual cost savings actions. The importance of this distinction is to provide clarity of action within the SCM group when determining individual work elements. The timing, implementation, and use of the cost management tools has a very different profile than the cost improvement actions.

ACT-based Sourcing

The importance of the affordable cost target (ACT) methodology in cost management is that the practice provides a direct link between procurement costs and individual program prof-

1. The economic increase due to labor and overhead changes are assumed never to be considered customer responsibility. Figure 13.3 shows offsets increasing due to raw material price changes, with increasing absorption based on greater contract coverage.

Commodity 2

Total current sources: 6				
Target # of sources: 2				
	2004	**2005**	**2006**	**2007**
# Suppliers	6	4	3	3
LTA Coverage	50%	65%	85%	100%
Annual Buy (000's)	$ -	$4,242,145	$5,765,512	$6,214,771
Forcasted Economic Exposure (FY04-08)				
Material:	$299,938	$176,921	$211,154	$176,921
Labor:	$102,636	$88,737	$78	$78
Overhead:	$111,433	$108,775	$95	$95
Total economic exposure	$514,007	$374,433	$211,327	$177,093
Forcasted annual buy + exposure	$514,007	$4,616,578	$5,976,839	$6,391,864

Planned Cost Savings and Avoidance

Savings:				
Net productivity 3.5%	$0	$96,509	$171,524	$217,517
Resourcing / negotiate 3.0%	$0	$82,722	$297,021	$186,443
Total savings	$0	$179,231	$468,545	$403,960
Avoidances:				
Material 5% cap	$149,969	$114,998	$179,481	$176,921
Labor	$102,636	$88,737	$78	$78
Overhead	$111,433	$108,775	$95	$95
Total avoidances	$364,038	$312,510	$179,654	$177,093
Total savings and avoidances	$364,038	$491,741	$648,198	$581,053
Net Fiscal Year Impact	$149,969	$(117,308)	$(436,871)	$(403,960)

Figure 13.3 LTA Impact

itability. The practice drives the internal organization and the supplier organizations to a price-based costing relationship. Through these efforts, the known affordable price determines the allowable costs and results in improvement and development efforts aimed at delivering the required cost levels. While the levels are not always achievable, they do provide a specific goal and not a generalized direction.

Many purchasing organizations are reluctant to use cost targets when quoting suppliers, often believing that the result may be higher quoted prices. This view of the target as the "floor" is generally incorrect. Where cost targets are realistically created, and where these targets are coupled with continued competitive quoting, the prices quoted often come in below the target. The target becomes the ceiling of the quotes received from the suppliers. The risk in this approach is often driven by financial organizations where the targets become so aggressive they do not reflect any real or achievable price. All credibility of the target pricing process can be lost, so SCM leaders need to take the lead role in maintaining the integrity of this process.

Supplier Development Cost Management

Chapter 12 outlined the performance improvement characteristics of a robust supplier development process. Equally important to the effects on quality, delivery, and responsiveness is the effect these actions have on cost improvement and management. While supplier quality efforts resolve immediate issues, supplier development efforts affect total performance. Most SCM organizations fail to recognize the financial impact that these efforts have and get caught up in fire fighting versus planning.

The breadth of the lean efforts described in this book can be applied to lower-tier suppliers. The problem becomes the availability of resources to define, train, and implement lean SCM action when total company revenues fall below (or never rise to) a level in which these support services can be afforded. Figure 13.4 represents an actual company experience where supplier development efforts were focused on systemic improvement. Although not perfect, as evidenced by increases

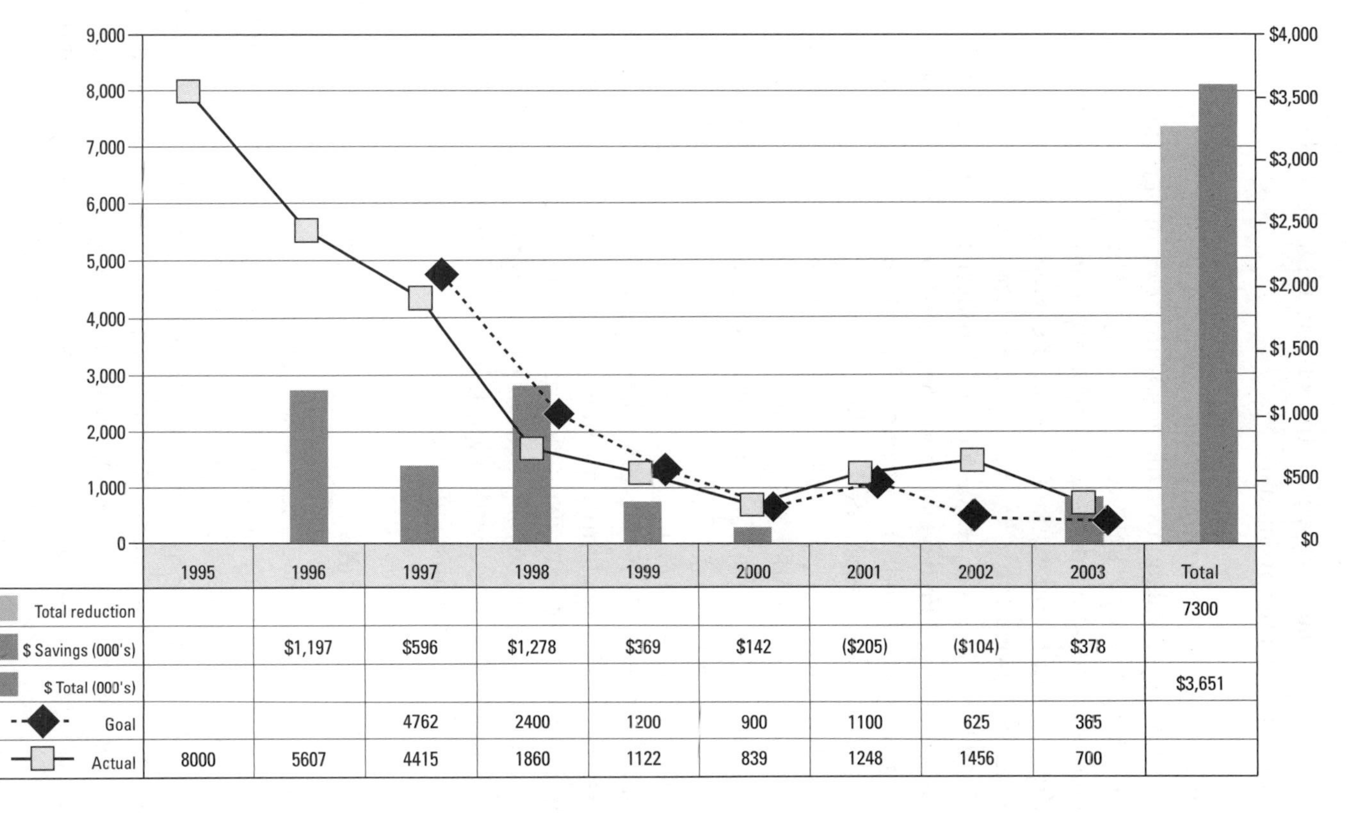

	1995	1996	1997	1998	1999	2000	2001	2002	2003	Total
Total reduction										7300
$ Savings (000's)		$1,197	$596	$1,278	$369	$142	($205)	($104)	$378	
$ Total (000's)										$3,651
Goal			4762	2400	1200	900	1100	625	365	
Actual	8000	5607	4415	1860	1122	839	1248	1456	700	

Figure 13.4 Supplier Quality/Cost Improvement

in PPM in the last two years, the efforts targeted a 50 percent year-over-year improvement.

The savings directed back to the supply base by these efforts are a simple calculation of the total turnover multiplied by the PPM rate, resulting in a reject savings. The internal impact includes these, plus detection and prevention costs, including customer return and warranty costs. The savings due to reduced quality rejections for a $5 billion annual buy would be nearly $33 million. The savings achieved through the efforts of the company's supplier development organization can be captured commercially through the incremental commodity and supplier specific objectives as defined earlier in this chapter. The internal inspection, detection, prevention, and warranty savings are easily equal to this amount. While not able to eliminate these internal tasks, the resource allocation to them can be reduced.

Reductions in supplier product nonconformance represent only a small portion of the development opportunities. Equivalent lower-tier savings actions are attainable, as well as the internal implementation of lean manufacturing techniques. The supplier development efforts, while focused on improved process, must not lose sight of the contribution the organization can make in overall SCM cost management activities.

3. COST TARGET SETTING

Among the cost management strategies described was the use of a cost target sourcing method. Rather than just viewing the targeting process as a tool, there must be recognition of the importance of setting the appropriate methodologies and usage, as well as an understanding of how to capture and manage the data for the greatest use. The cost management information and the price benchmarking in the crisis section discussed how and why to use a target process. This section details what to capture and what to do with the information.

Supply Data Warehouse

The target development process that was shown in Chapter 6 provides individual definition for each program and program bill of materials. Also important to the process is the development of a surrogate data base as shown in Figure 6.1. A supplier cost database in which like parts drive a surrogate starting point, ensures a commonality of price targets and continued improvement through incremental cost reductions. The need to capture past work as a basis for current and future pricing efforts requires the ease of reference that such a data base can provide. Through e-business and e-procurement tools, data management or data mining allow financial goal setting for future programs to be based on realistic product costing and cost improvement assumptions.

DFA/DFM Modeling

Design for assembly and design for manufacturing models provide the ability to link product design features to production efficiencies. This link extends the concept of supply chain management into value chain management by recognizing the constraints in manufacturing efficiencies and design's contribution to these constraints. Motorola's early work in Six Sigma was centered on the effects of design on production quality conformance. Like the efforts in supplier development, improvements gained and retained through DFA/DFM work contribute to cost structure improvement.

DFA/DFM modeling packages generally include economic factors related to specific material and labor usage, overhead costs for specific manufacturing processes, and assembly complexity factors to derive additional assembly level cost or price targets. In conjunction with the supply data warehouse surrogates and cost targeting process, these various pieces of data provide the broadest level of pricing data available for the determination of program level financial performance targets. The actual versus forecasted performance to the DFA/DFM objectives provides additional data with which to capture and retain design and manufacturing improvements.

Logic Model Sourcing

Logic model sourcing is a colorful way to say that sourcing is based on more factors than price. By using multidimensional data factors, including cost, quality performance, delivery performance, and others, sourcing decisions are made which support the widest scope of organizational needs at the best value. Price is only a single factor of the sourcing decision.

Figure 13.5 is one such logic-based sourcing model. In addition to the various cost factors and relation to target pricing, the model includes transportation factors through proximity measures and other supply chain factors. The decision is driven through a variable scoring method to specifically defined stratification standards. In addition, the sourcing model provides a recapitulation summary in which appropriate sourcing approval can be secured. This provides a single format in which multiple supply and value chain elements can be evaluated, as well as providing a variable weighting scheme to accurately reflect the variations in commodity requirements and sensitivity.

4. VALUE MANAGEMENT

Value management (VM) broadly defines the various efforts to capture and retain improvements at each step of the value and supply chain. Cost management, supplier management, logistics management, design management, and manufacturing management all have elements attributed to value management. Well-known tools exist in each of these, and when utilized as part of an overarching operating philosophy create a change- and improvement-focused organization. In SCM, value management becomes the most significant intersection of the internal customer organizations that SCM supports. Organizational success

Part Sourcing Matrix

Target Price: ____________ Part Number: ____________ Part Name: ____________

	Weight	40%	20%	5%	10%	5%	20%		
Supplier	Price	Cost	Quality	Location	Productivity	Payment	Delivery	Total Points	Remarks
		Ev. 0	Ev. 0	Ev. 0	Ev. 0	Ev. 0	Ev. 0		
		Pts. 0	Pts. 0	Pts. 0	Pts. 0	Pts. 0	Pts. 0	0.0	
		Ev. 0	Ev. 0	Ev. 0	Ev. 0	Ev. 0	Ev. 0		
		Pts. 0	Pts. 0	Pts. 0	Pts. 0	Pts. 0	Pts. 0	0.0	
		Ev. 0	Ev. 0	Ev. 0	Ev. 0	Ev. 0	Ev. 0		
		Pts. 0	Pts. 0	Pts. 0	Pts. 0	Pts. 0	Pts. 0	0.0	
		Ev. 0	Ev. 0	Ev. 0	Ev. 0	Ev. 0	Ev. 0		
		Pts. 0	Pts. 0	Pts. 0	Pts. 0	Pts. 0	Pts. 0	0.0	
		Ev. 0	Ev. 0	Ev. 0	Ev. 0	Ev. 0	Ev. 0		
		Pts. 0	Pts. 0	Pts. 0	Pts. 0	Pts. 0	Pts. 0	0.0	
		Ev. 0	Ev. 0	Ev. 0	Ev. 0	Ev. 0	Ev. 0		
		Pts. 0	Pts. 0	Pts. 0	Pts. 0	Pts. 0	Pts. 0	0.0	
To be seen by Manager Director VP Purchasing		Critera Relation to price target. If no target or cost estimate use lowest price quote	Critera 1 ppm = 100 63 ppm = 90 318 ppm = 80 2700 ppm = 70 >2700 ppm = 60	Critera 0 – 1 = 100 100 – 250 = 95 250 – 500 = 90 500 – 750 = 80 750 – 1500 = 70 1500 + = 60	Critera >5% = 100 4.5 – 5% = 90 3.5 – 4.5% = 80 2.5 – 3.5% = 70 1 – 2.5% = 60 0 – 1% = 50	Critera 60 prox = 100 45 prox = 90 30 prox = 80 Net 30/disc = 70 N et 30 = 60	Critera Enter delivery rating from most recent period	100 + Rating = Best 0 Rating = Unsuitable Date ________ Signature ________	

Figure 13.5 Logic Sourcing Matrix

is based on integrating internal and external relationships by creating a seamless organization. Many professionals define value as function/cost (V=F/C).

Value Stream Mapping

Value steam mapping is a visual process developed to provide an analysis tool that defines operational inefficiencies as well as ideal end state maps. In the book *Learning to See*, Mike Rother and John Shook provide a simple methodology for examining the internal value stream within an operation.[2] Jim Womack and Dan Jones defined the methods in which to expand this effort to the entire value chain in their book *Seeing the Whole: Mapping the Extended Value Stream*.[3] The extended value stream is often synonymous with value chain, the difference in focus being a high-level initial evaluation in the relationship dynamics between the players in the chain in the value chain focus.[4]

Value stream mapping disciplines provide a roadmap on efficiency opportunities to which SCM organizations can develop continuous improvement plans and work to identify an ideal end state. The opportunities identified through the mapping process are incorporated into the lean SCM practices and overarching corporate objectives to create a detailed strategic plan and individual performance objectives.

VA/VE Workshops

Value analysis and value engineering workshops are focused value management tools used to improve design related cost structures. However, for VA/VE efforts to have long-lasting

---

2. Mike Rother and John Shook, *Learning to See*, Lean Enterprise Institure Inc; (December 1999).
3. Dan Jones and James P Womack, *Seeing the Whole: Mapping the Extended Value Stream*, Lean Enterprise Institute Inc; Spiral edition (November 2002).
4. Hazel A. Beck, Value Innovations Ltd.

effectiveness, short-term VA efforts must be coordinated with long-term VE efforts. To accomplish this, VA and VE must be a jointly managed effort, with specific product, commodity, or supplier initiatives capturing the data for current and future applications.

Value Data Management

Similar to supplier data management, value data management is critical in retaining the learned improvements. Through formal linkage efforts, actions taken in design, process, logistics, and other value factors can be directly associated with specific teams, suppliers, parts, or programs. The importance of this effort is to eliminate the three steps forward, two steps back reality that often happens during points of transition. The points of transition can either be changes in programs or designs from one generation to the next; changes in personnel, whether supply chain, engineering, program management or other; changes in sourcing; or any of a hundred other change factors. The integration and management of data in value management has been greatly simplified with the advancement of software solutions dedicated to enterprise intelligence. Companies such as SAS[5] provide technology solutions for data analytics and business intelligence. Software and service providers such as i2, Ariba, Baan, and others offer similar data management products.

The management of the value management data ultimately needs to be driven back to the SCM of individual supplier performance. The final chapter in the value management efforts is the integration of performance back into supplier and customer

5. SAS Institute is a leading supplier in data analytics. Many of its platforms are dedicated to capturing and managing performance and intelligence data to support decision making. Information on supplier relationship management and data analytic tools from SAS can be found at www.sas.com.

expectations. It is only though this coordination that the efforts transcend individual tasks to become living processes. Previously defined stratification measures and annual improvement targets define the process in which this performance can be included.

5. SUPPLY CHAIN PROCESS IMPROVEMENT

In our discussion of cost management, one of the opportunities identified was the incorporation of supplier development actions to drive cost improvement. In most of these supplier development actions, the focus is on individual suppliers and supplier processes. Just as *Seeing the Whole* was an expansion of *Learning to See*, the efforts of supplier development can also be expanded. In addition to improving discrete processes, supplier development should also focus on improving the supply chain process. Through the use of kaizen and kaikaku tools, suppliers and customers can gain improvements in the ways in which business is conducted, not just in the application of the lean SCM tools.

This chapter calls for integration of data into business practices. Likewise, the performance and business practices have to be incorporated into the overall business system described throughout this book—such as the MBP process. The performance in cost containment should reflect the individual contributor actions, the departmental objectives, and ultimately the overarching objectives. Without evidence of direct contribution to these goals, a reevaluation of the performance, of the objectives, or of SCM practices must occur. The nature of the work and the effort of the work must provide the results that are determined to be the most beneficial to the company.

SUMMARY

Cost management and cost control are often the exclusive focus of a supply chain organization, and even more so of procurement within SCM. The ability to achieve financial improvement in SCM requires efforts affecting the entire value chain and relies on the efforts of nonprocurement resources (such as supplier development and engineering).

Financial improvement in the supply chain is a reality of modern business. The approaches to achieve these savings need to be structured, reliable, and based on ethical business relationships. As described in Chapter 3, being hard on the issues (such as price improvement) is acceptable in business, provided the basis of the relationship includes a delineation of business requirements and ramifications.

CASE STUDY 13.2

Questions

1. In what ways could the supply chain organization contribute to the cost management and cost improvement of the company?
2. Why was the SCM group unable to articulate the full level of savings contribution that was being made? What could be done differently to better articulate the full scope of savings?
3. DSW's VP of Supply Chain Management was concerned about the overemphasis on the financial impact of the SCM contributions. What can be done to alleviate these concerns?

Answers

1. The supply chain organization had developed and implemented plans to provide hard cost savings (i.e., documented cost reductions) in both production and nonproduction materials through the use of price targeting and consolidation

efforts. The consolidation targets were based on the use of comparative benchmarking assessments. Immediate resourcing based savings and commitments to ongoing price reductions were achieved during the consolidation activities.

Soft cost savings (i.e., cost avoidances, administrative cost reductions, etc.) were developed and implemented in supplier development activities, especially related to variation reduction and supplier-based part per million (PPM) reject reductions. These savings were translated into a hard number contribution equivalent, including labor-related savings as measured by full time equivalents (FTEs).

The hard and soft cost savings totals were related to overall contribution to DSW in terms of earnings per share (EPS). DSW had 150 million outstanding shares of stock, so each $1,000,000 in savings = $.006 EPS. Therefore, savings of $50,000,000 = $.30 EPS. This measure could be directly compared to EPS contribution due to incremental sales and other cost reduction activities, and allow for a valued assessment of SCM efforts.

2. Initially the SCM organization did not quantify the nonprocurement savings it was achieving. The focus of the effort was on the underlying improvements in quality and other supply chain activities. Quantifying the value of these improvements was secondary to the efforts and actual improvements made.

   Ultimately the SCM was able to articulate the full scope of savings by translating the value of soft savings into hard savings equivalents. By benchmarking the ratio of overhead cost supporting supply chain management to the total savings level, the organization was able to show the competitive value it contributed to the organization.

3. The concern of DSW's VP of Supply Chain Management was that the overemphasis on the financial impact would divert the efforts from delivering improvement to reporting improvement. Where the sole measure of success becomes financial measures, individuals within the organization find creative methods to make those measures look good. One actual incident occurred when a purchasing manager allowed buyers to issue purchase orders at a price higher than the quote, only to receive the overage rebated at the end of the year. The purpose of this was to achieve the increasing financial objectives.

   The concerns were lessened by the use of balanced performance measures in which financial evaluation was one of five measures. The use of balanced measures through hoshin planning enabled the organization to recognize the value of financial measures equal to other quality, cost, and delivery indicators. Increased audit and governance was put in place to discourage creative reporting and goal attainment.

14

Materials Management

DISTRIBUTION, TRANSPORTATION, AND CUSTOMER SERVICE

The distribution, transportation, and order fulfillment impacting physical product movement often defines supply chain management. While in reality supply chain management is much more, these elements undoubtedly exist. In lean supply chain management, the implementation of these efforts as a strategic initiative involves the incorporation of elements of lean manufacturing systems. Here, the objective is not only the successful movement of the product, but also the implementation of highly visual and efficient systems by and through which the product is moved.

Like the efforts of supplier development described in the last two chapters, materials management provides for the opportunity of improved performance, including cost reductions. Recognizing this aspect of supply chain management as an equal contributor to overall lean efforts and success addresses the last element of the value chain. However, in addition to the product movement and order fulfillment is the added responsibility of customer service. While perhaps difficult to define in so many industries with so many varying demands, customer service and satisfaction is becoming an increasing supply chain responsibility.

This chapter describes the integration of lean methodologies into materials handling and management activities. Process and cost improvements continue to be the basis on which the strategic initiatives are built.

STRATEGIC MATERIALS MANAGEMENT

The strategic materials initiative is geared toward three primary elements. The first element is to develop a visual factory-like structure using fixed inventory locations. The second is to distinguish distribution operations from warehousing and storage operations to create material efficiency measures. The third element is to provide for improved transportation costs.

Strategic Initiative

The strategic initiative here is to maximize order fill rate and reaction time for all end item components. The goal should also be to increase warehouse facility utilization to enable incoming consignment opportunities and to integrate logistic operations (transportation, distribution, and customer service) into a single multidisciplinary activity.

Implementation Plan

The following elements make up the implementation plan for this initiative:

- *Inventory flow and storage*:
    1. Establish visual factory inventory management.
    2. With production operations, establish min/max kanban production pull methodology.
    3. Identify fixed inventory locations for high use items.
    4. Dedicate customer lanes for product inventory, staging, and distribution.

CASE STUDY 14.1

Customer order entry through EDI (electronic data interchange) release comes into DSW through its distribution operations. All orders from its automotive, aerospace, and defense customers are then processed to the individual manufacturing centers. Regional distribution centers consolidate products for staging and mixed-load shipping. DSW maintained a regional delivery fleet and a limited national over-the-road delivery fleet. Various product configuration and order requirements allow direct full truckload shipments, other are mixed loads with multiple part numbers. Inventory storage is based on free location managed through bar-coding (free location meaning storage to any open inventory location).

Distribution operations have appeared to max out space availability, yet often seem to be short of the required components needed to complete shipments. Customer requirements allow for changes of shipment up to two hours prior to pick-up time. Delivery is often sequenced orders for color and configuration as well as just-in-time frequencies.

Questions

1. What lean techniques can be borrowed from the manufacturing environment to aid in the efficient operations in DSW's distribution operations?
2. How could DSW improve overall material management operations in an effort to improve order fulfillment rates?
3. What measures would best represent the pace of improvements within the distribution operations given the delivery pattern?

- *Facility use*:
  1. Eliminate excess returnable rack inventory through evaluation and customer return.
  2. Streamline material flow methods to eliminate redundant movement.
  3. Manage space allocation by customer-driven demands.
  4. Evaluate direct ship and space lease opportunities.
- *Logistics integration*:
  1. Create customer service and distribution teams in lieu of functional segregation and product alignment.
  2. Identify a single point logistics manager.
  3. Incorporate release through shipment planning as a single material management function.

Each of these elements is examined in more detail in the following sections.

1. INVENTORY FLOW AND STORAGE

Distribution operations are frequently a hive of activity representing controlled chaos. Automated systems often provide relief from error through automated pick systems. These systems economically apply to high-volume distribution systems exhibiting common packaging configurations. Distribution operations with vastly different package sizes and lot frequencies don't always lend themselves to automated systems, nor do lower-volume operations.

Visual factory techniques (where product and facilities are bound to specific locations and volumes) provide a calming effect to the transactions, quantities, and locations of materials within the distribution operations. By more precisely managing the storage and movement of material, a closer relationship can be established between the production operations and distribution and customer demand. Manufacturing scheduling control and refinement can be managed through visual verification of demand fluctuation, which may not be captured in automated information systems. Whereas retail consumer product demand and delivery systems can provide accurate real-time demand changes, industrial manufacturing for nonretail customers have not benefited from the same systems.

The first step in visual factory implementation is the distribution equivalent of the manufacturing marketplace. In manufacturing, raw material and components are stored in fixed inventory locations with limited inventory capacity. Similarly, finished goods storage is fixed to a specific physical location address and limited in quantity stored. Minimum and maximum (min/max) inventory levels are established based upon customer demand analysis and production capabilities—such as order response and production lead time. Any spillage above the max level provides a signal back to operations to curtail production or to reassess production schedule methods. Shortages beyond minimum provide a similar evaluation point.

When implemented to its ultimate application, the management to the marketplace min/max levels can provide production pull signals to manufacturing. The use of kanban signals based on the distribution requirements provides the closest link between actual demand and production. Demand and lot size planning disciplines used in planning for raw material and component acquisition applies similarly in this scenario. The kanban signals can be cards, electronic, or many other formats as supported by the logistics or manufacturing network configuration.

2. FACILITY USE

Facility form (i.e., the physical structure and its use) often does not match the function for which it is used. For example, in industries where the majority of demand is unique to each customer, the inventory storage and management often reflect product type and not customer. This typically results in excessive or redundant product move to re-aggregate the parts by customer. Order picking and staging becomes a complex network of people and assets. In contrast, if storage and processing in these industries is based on customer demand and usage—inventory, staging, and shipment are more efficient, resulting in improved labor usage and lowered total cost.

Actual physical space allocation provides the lean interface between the distribution facility and the manufacturing site. Where facility allocation is determined by part level demand and arranged by customer, control over supply versus demand match is reinforced. Continuing to support the visual factory concept, total customer demand trends are more easily recognized by this facility allocation method. Low value and slow moving items also gain increased attention because of the availability (or lack of) valuable distribution space.

Finally, unless significant incremental sales warrant a need for increased distribution space, facility availability should be viewed as limited and unobtainable. This view requires continued improvements in efficiency and planning. The time from distribution receipt to shipment staging and transaction should continually be reduced. In some circumstances, distribution does not have to mean a physical transfer of parts from the manufacturing operation, but can mean virtual distribution handling from direct manufacturing site to customer shipments. The industrial sector drop-ship approach still has the ability to serve the efficiency efforts in consolidated product response and customer order fulfillment.

3. LOGISTICS INTEGRATION

Professional program and project management has provided a good example of how logistics operations can be integrated as part of the supply chain effort. In program management, a single manager oversees and coordinates the efforts of various functional employees to deliver a single product to the customer. The functional "chimneys" are broken down to deliver the best product and product value to the customer in a team environment.

Logistic integration as part of materials management and SCM can benefit from the same approach. Traditionally, distribution managers, shipping managers, and scheduling managers individually manage the various functional tasks. By re-creating the view of logistics operations, customer order fulfillment and satisfaction can be improved through a single point view of the materials tasks.

As a single point leader for the various functions, the logistics manager facilitates all materials efforts from order receipt through delivery, providing the customer one face for all issues. In addition, the logistics team leader becomes the single point liaison for internal contact as well. With this second role the individual customer-based needs identified by the organization can be captured and implemented uniformly throughout the logistic stream. Logistics managers from various customer teams can share best practices to improve all materials efforts.

THE RESULTS

Like the quality, cost, and delivery improvements in SCM, materials management also provides measurable improvements. The most obvious of these is reduction in transportation costs. Transportation rate negotiations, routing efficiencies, and move frequency are all contributors to this area of cost savings. When a materials organization focuses only on cost, manufacturing efficiencies can be disrupted. This is especially true in routing and frequency considerations. As pointed out in one of the early chapters, the competing improvement objectives in operational efficiency (such as lower inventory) and reduced costs must be consciously considered when working to optimize total cost structures. A balance must be struck between the potentially competing objectives. Cost savings in rate, routing, and frequency can easily range between 8 to 15 percent from traditional cost levels.

Perhaps not so obvious are the savings from the facility and visual factory changes. Many distribution facilities rely solely on computerized storage data accessible through RF (radio frequency) bar code scanning to manage inventory availability and placement. The approach often results in a random storage of product, with storage locations selected simply by whatever open space is available. In these cases, load picking and staging can often represent a chaotic, random walk throughout the facility in which multiple and distant inventory locations must be accessed for the same part. By utilizing visual storage methods, shipment staging times can be reduced by more than 25 percent, resulting in labor savings and increasing order fulfillment rates with a fixed labor force. Through the fixed and sequenced storage of inventory, manual pick operations become more controlled and efficient. Often the pick list can be sequenced to coordinate with the storage location so that a single progression within the warehouse can occur, eliminating backtracking.

Computer-based inventory management or other nonvisual methods can result in inaccurate inventory counts, creating customer shortages when shipments are staged. Because inventory can exist in random locations, any system failure or processing oversight has no way to flag potential shortages. Within a visual environment, the management of fixed inventory and min/max storage levels can likewise improve short shipments to customers by 50 percent or more. The efficiency gained in pick-stage-load operations by eliminating work interruptions can be significant. The magnitude of this savings is based on the rate of occurrence, and reaction procedure, but is typically equal to 15 percent of associated labor cost.

Each of these materials management efforts either directly or indirectly support the efficiency of the manufacturing operations. By limiting inventory space, the manufacturing operations can more accurately produce product to actual demand. By eliminating part shortages, the material management activity cannot "exercise" the organization to immediately respond and shift production priorities—enabling fixed production schedules. Other similar improvements can be defined throughout the materials management efforts and can provide links to overarching objectives of financial performance and customer satisfaction.

CASE STUDY 14.2

Questions

1. What lean techniques can be borrowed from the manufacturing environment to aid in the efficient operations in DSW's distribution operations?
2. How could DSW improve overall material management operations in an effort to improve order fulfillment rates?
3. What measures would best represent the pace of improvements within the distribution operations given the delivery pattern?

Answers

1. DSW implemented three primary lean efforts: 1) visual factory with fixed min/max inventory levels, 2) kanban pull signals from finished goods delivery, providing production scheduling per lean manufacturing structure, and 3) local delivery assets used as a heijunka pace setter driving receipt to staging time reductions.

2. DWS completed facility and organization changes to create customer-based teams, each with a single team leader. The teams and facilities became responsible for all multifunctional logistics and materials management activities. By having a materials "cradle to grave" owner, the company created "subject matter" or customer experts who could provide a greater focus on individual customer needs. Likewise, the facility was organized so that all customer product was located in dedicated and contiguous warehouse space, enabling the use of various lean management tools.

3. Customer satisfaction was generally driven by order fulfillment. However, due to the frequency of shipments, and need for part sequencing, stringent measures in excess of customer demand were put into place. Shipments that did not contain the appropriate mix or quantity of parts on a specific truck, but were delivered during the same day, were counted against the material and plant performance indicators.

   This measure of "shortships" generally was far tougher than the customer measures, which required shipment within the one day delivery window. Like other measures at DSW, this and more were incorporated as the hoshin planning measures for the materials operations.

15

The Supply Chain Organization

This final chapter of Section III is a brief discussion of the organizational fit between the strategic lean supply chain efforts and the resources available to deploy them. Any structure can be successful, whether single line, matrix, functional, operational, etc. Required skills and training are far more important than the reporting structure in which they reside. Lean supply chain management requires a vastly different set of skills from traditional supply chain management. Lean supply chain management requires both the technical ability related to lean supply chain initiatives as well as the relationship skills with which to deploy them to the supply base.

Organizational Structure

Organizational structure is seldom considered a strategic initiative, except perhaps in the human resources department. In SCM the strategic initiative is based on the value a particular organizational structure and skills training provides.

Strategic Initiative

The strategic initiative here is to enhance the capability and efficiency of the supply chain organization by developing lean-based improvement strategies within procurement, supplier

CASE STUDY 15.1

Concurrent to the launch of its initial lean supply chain efforts, DSW had entered into a companywide organizational assessment. In an effort to improve its functional performance, increase customer satisfaction, and improve profits, DSW was striving to understand what appropriate changes should be made.

Operationally the company had very strong and independent divisions, each possessing its own functional organizations. A small corporate staff served to mediate the differences in functional practices between the organizations, and was now being asked to take a more direct role in these efforts.

Questions

1. Under what organizational structure could DSW's supply chain organization increase its lean supply chain efforts through synergy of effort and resources, while maintaining the divisional independence and control?
2. How would the SCM organization insure its employees possess the appropriate skills necessary to initiate lean supply chain efforts, and how would it plan for promotions and succession?
3. What arguments might be expected from the divisional general managers and the supply chain employees against a revised SCM structure, and how would the SCM group counter these arguments?

development, and materials management, thereby increasing the focus on the strategic management of information and communications (via e-business systems) to support supply base management and customer service requirements. This can be done by implementing training methods to support the achievement of business plan initiatives and overarching hoshin objectives, highlighting action deployment and sustained improvement.

At fully staffed levels, salary structure needs should be evaluated, and opportunities to consolidate or restructure responsibilities to improve needed budget allocation should be identified. Global purchasing requirements can be integrated into a single worldwide procurement strategy or organization.

Implementation Plan

The following elements make up the implementation plan for this strategic initiative:

- *Organization (see Table 15.1):*
    1. Assess resource deployment and determine appropriate program team support while continuing to optimize core competencies.
    2. Focus purchasing and supplier development resources on developing a supply base that provides a competitive advantage in cost, quality, and technology.
    3. Focus materials and logistics resources on effective inventory management and customer order fulfillment.
    4. Facilitate benchmarking, supplier development, and strategic analysis using data analysis tools.
    5. Define global purchasing strategies and staffing needs.
- *People:*
    1. Develop training curriculum and courses for all job classifications.
    2. Develop gap analysis skills evaluation for all employees (including team leaders and managers).
    3. Expand training for supervisors to focus on leadership, employee training, skill enhancement, and successor planning.

Table 15.1 Organization Alternatives

Activity	Current Structure	Proposed Structure
Global procurement operations	No formal global organization—regional functional focus only	International procurement manager to coordinate efforts and opportunities
Supplier development	Quality-based, procurement dependent structure	Development-based, procurement supportive organization. Commodity and discipline expertise
Distribution, transportation and customer service	Functionally driven separate activities—"chimney organizations"	Customer-based logistics teams—incorporated materials functions

THE ORGANIZATION EFFORTS

In any business environment, a team-based structure provides the greatest opportunity to deliver the desired results and changes. Individual teams allow for a sense of entrepreneurial spirit even in classic corporate environments. By breaking the walls of functional responsibility, team members share hats in job assignments. All members have a shared equity in the success or failure of the project, and therefore break from the normal "not-my-job" mentality.

The organizational development of a lean supply chain team must carefully consider the ways in which limited human resources can be most appropriately applied in a global organization to optimize performance. Targeting resources often means moving people outside of their functional comfort zone.

PROCUREMENT AND DEVELOPMENT

In supporting lean SCM, procurement and development resources need to be initially targeted on the development of supply base capabilities. While this often conflicts with the desire for immediate cost reductions, it provides long-term sustainability of reduction efforts (as discussed in previous chapters). Global coordination of procurement and supplier development efforts needs to include a recognition of the varying social and political environments in which the businesses operate.

Through a global analytical assessment, tailored regional commodity deployments maximize systemwide benefits. The use of global commodity managers (or lead buyer structures) allows for a balance between tactical and development responsibilities as well as the consideration of specific regional deployment needs. In any region, the global application of lean supply chain elements facilitates the competitive and price benchmarking efforts leading to a consolidated commodity strategy. Supplier and commodity development activities arising out of these evaluation tools create the basis for globally coordinated efforts. Internal and external organizations quickly recognize the single-voice approach between operations, divisions, and world regions, minimizing the divide-and-conquer efforts suppliers often exhibit.

MATERIALS MANAGEMENT

Material and logistics staff, again organized as teams, are directed in the management and integration of lean techniques in support of inventory management and reduction, along with improved order fulfillment. Chapter 14 provided the applications of the techniques to this staffing structure. The operational efficiencies gained through lean deployment can be quantified to support total supply chain savings.

When various materials management activities, such as production planning, logistics, transportation, and customer service are integrated, the organization deconstructs the functional inefficiency typically exhibited in material movement activities. Focus shifts from individual tasks to customer satisfaction. The tasks are designed to support broad customer satisfaction and therefore construct a new paradigm toward job performance.

PEOPLE AND SKILL DEVELOPMENT

Key to the successful delivery of lean SCM initiatives is the capable workforce to do so. It is unlikely that most organizations already possess the developed lean supply chain skills outlined in this book. To develop those skills, the supply chain manager must provide specific knowledge and training requirements and have the ability to measure competency within those skill sets. Through the development of a skills and development matrix as shown in Figure 15.1, the supply chain manager can clearly articulate to his or her staff and to the broader organization the level of mastery of lean SCM. Figure 15.1 categorizes skills by areas of mastery—e-technology skills, business development skills, and lean knowledge skills. Within each of these skill sets, the required level of mastery is defined, along with the evaluated level of each of the employees. The deviation of these two indicators provides the gap assessment that drives employee development.

Coupling experience and performance with skill mastery creates the environment in which fact-based succession planning can be derived. By formal use of skills mastery and annual performance reviews, each successive level of job classification can identify a successor or promotional opportunity. Through this, each employee can be certain of the path he or she is on, and where he or she needs to head to progress in his or her career. As there are many forms of succession planning methods, this book will not offer a new one. Selecting and using one that is already known will satisfy your organization's skill development needs.

SUMMARY

This chapter has provided a quick glimpse of the need to consciously address organizational coordination to support lean

Team Leader							Master
0. What is it? 1. Know 2. Understand 3. Use 4. Mastered 5. Teach ☐ Needs development ◯ Can teach others	Employee 1	Employee 2	Employee 3				*Place team members names here* ← **Team Development Strategies**
Technology Skills							
Word (3)	3	3	3				
Excel (3)	3	3	3				
Electronic communications (3)	4	3	3				
MRP/planning (3)	3	1	3				
ERP/order management (3)	1	1	3				
Development Skills							
Strategic planning (3)	3	3	3				
Goal setting/MBP — Hoshin Planning (4)	3	3	2				Team attend the MBP training
Leadership training	3	3	3				
Presentation skills (4)	4	3	3				
Meeting facilitation (4)	4	3	3				
Project management (3)	3	2	3				
Financial management (3)	3	2	2				Develop financial workshop
Communication	4	3	3				
Interpersonal	3	3	3				
Problem solving (3)	3	2	2				Distribute fact based p/s workbook
Price benchmarking (3)	3	2	2				
Knowledge							
SPC/PPM reduction (2)	2	2	2				
Quality systems (3)	3	2	3				
Lean manufacturing (3)	3	2	3				
QS9000/TS16949 (5)	5	3	3				
Program management (3)	3	2	3				Develop PMP purchasing training class
Supplier benchmarking (5)	5	2	4				
Negotiations (4)	5	3	4				
Price Benchmarking (3)	3	2	2				

Figure 15.1 Skills Matrix

supply chain needs. Not only does the traditional organizational design need to take place, but, more important, the analysis of actual employee skill to required skill level must be done. Training and education in these lean elements are more important than the structure in which they operate. Finally, succession planning needs to occur to ensure adequate "bench strength" in the SCM organization. By specifically targeting needed training elements, an SCM staff can be created that has the ability to operate in any of the many supply chain positions.

CASE STUDY 15.2

Questions

1. Under what organizational structure could DSW's supply chain organization increase its lean supply chain efforts through synergy of effort and resources, while maintaining the divisional independence and control?
2. How would the SCM organization insure its employees possess the appropriate skills necessary to initiate lean supply chain efforts, and how would it plan for promotions and succession?
3. What arguments might be expected from the divisional general managers and the supply chain employees against a revised SCM structure, and how would the SCM group counter these arguments?

Answers

1. DSW employed a "hybrid" organization in which tactical or functional SCM remained fully within the operating division, and a strategic supply chain group was formed as part of the corporate function. The centralized group was

responsible for the selection and development of all long-term suppliers; was the lead negotiator for all multiyear agreements; was responsible for cross-division commodity group savings; and acted as a commodity council leader for all divisions that purchased a particular commodity. The corporate SCM executive was responsible for the performance assessment, job assignment, and development of all SCM personnel. Daily job reporting was determined by employee deployment, with divisional managers responsible for functionally deployed SCM personnel. While not a matrix organization with dual formal reporting relationships, DSW's hybrid organization relied on the daily manager (whether tactical or strategic) to provide performance direction and evaluation.

2. The SCM management team identified the curriculum of necessary skills for all positions and all levels. Each manager completed a skills assessment for each employee and developed an individualized training plan. The general training matrix outlined not only the required and recommended skills for each position, but provided a clear indication of the skills required at all levels, so that employees could pursue the skills required for promotional opportunities. Finally, the individualized training matrix was used as part of the annual performance review process.

3. The divisional general managers expressed concern with what was perceived as a loss of control for a major cost element of their profit and loss responsibilities. By having the commodity level savings performance targeted by, and controlled by, the centralized supply chain group, the general managers felt that they would not receive the attention necessary for them to meet or exceed their profitability targets.

The SCM executive explained that the product sourcing would occur within the division, with the tactical buyer negotiating the initial price. The strategic group was responsible for using SCM tools, such as multiyear productivity agreements, VA improvements, etc., to ensure continual cost reduction activity. Additionally, the strategic group would also provide extended supplier development support to assist the divisions with their most problematic suppliers, allowing the divisional quality resources to focus on internal and customer quality improvements.

Other concerns included determination of resource levels and personnel deployment, performance evaluations, pay and promotion decisions, concern over conflicting directives from the divisions and the central organization; etc. Each of these issues had to be addressed with an ongoing dialogue between the divisional managers and the corporate managers. It required recognition that each of the groups was striving to provide the best results for the benefit of the entire company. Once the ego control issues were put aside and the common efforts recognized, both teams were able to successfully operate within the new organization. The most significant key element in "forcing" the facilitation and resolution of the concerns was executive corporate support and their championing of the concept of lean supply chain initiatives. The company's highest management recognized and endorsed the importance of the contribution SCM could make.

The SCM employees expressed only two main concerns: 1) to whom would they report; and 2) how would they be measured on performance? The first of these was addressed by clearly defining that when deployed in an operational position, they would report directly to the divisional manager who would determine "what and when" supply chain activities needed to be undertaken. The issue of "who and how" the supply chain job was to be done was under the direction of the corporate supply chain manager. The performance issue mirrored the reporting issue in that the corporate manager was ultimately responsible for the performance evaluation. However, when operationally deployed, 50 percent of the evaluation was based on operation performance as determined by the operational manager.

After initial concern, the employees embraced the new organization as it allowed for a better match between skills and job tasks. Employees who excelled in the operational and tactical side of supply chain management were relieved of the distractions of attempting to define strategic initiatives. Likewise, SCM strategists were provided an environment in which they could focus on long-term initiatives without the daily interruptions of production support issues. The organization also provided for job rotation and development, allowing for movement between various divisions as well as tactical and strategic assignments.

SECTION IV

Coordinating SCM and Lean Management

16

Developing & Implementing Lean Fundamentals

All the material presented so far loosely assumes that lean manufacturing techniques are already in place, enabling the launch of lean supply chain efforts. Section IV shows how to implement internal lean manufacturing efforts and lean supply chain activities simultaneously. This is accomplished by pairing the internal implementation steps with supplier readiness steps. The following material takes the basic lean manufacturing initiatives and matches those efforts to supply chain support initiatives. The in-depth focus is on the supply chain aspects of this pairing, not on the lean manufacturing aspects.

IMPLEMENTING THE MATERIALS FLOW STRATEGY

The first real coordination effort between the launch of lean manufacturing and SCM is in the materials flow strategy. It's at this starting point that the procurement activities have to be ready to support manufacturing's first steps toward lean implementation. The following sections show the correlation between the lean initiatives and SCM activities.

LEAN ACTION 1

Like the manufacturing process itself, the implementation of lean manufacturing techniques can be followed as material

CASE STUDY 16.1

DSW's North American operations began the implementation of lean manufacturing methods approximately 18 months prior to the development of the lean supply chain efforts. Many of the key elements were beginning to take hold, however, supplier performance in quality and delivery had seemed to deteriorate. As driven by the lean manufacturing efforts, delivery frequency was increasing while lot sizes and on-hand inventory were decreasing.

The rest of the DSW's worldwide organizations had yet to implement the lean manufacturing efforts, and were just beginning implementation plans. Customer demands for cost reductions and quality improvements were driving DSW toward a more rapid implementation than had occurred in North America. Additionally, a recent "noncore" acquisition was causing a serious financial drain on the entire company, both limiting the available cash for improvement initiatives and requiring immediate cost reductions.

Questions

1. Based on DSW's worldwide lean implantation efforts and progress, and its current financial situation, where should DSW focus its SCM efforts, and in what areas?
2. Based on the implementation focus, what impact might DSW see in commonizing a global approach to lean SCM efforts?
3. How would the SCM organization get in step with the North American lean manufacturing efforts?

flows into the plant. A materials flow strategy begins with the receipt and storage of raw material and components. Before any discussions begin regarding JIT deliveries, line-side shipments, etc., raw material and component storage processes must be established. In a lean manufacturing environment, this material storage is based on the concept of marketplace material storage.

In this marketplace concept, each received material or component has it own highly visible storage location, much like that in a grocery store. The purpose of this method is to precisely manage the location and movement into the manufacturing environment. However, Rother and Shook in *Learning to See* caution about the use of supermarket pull systems between processes until continuous flow has been introduced in as many processes as possible.[1] What I am proposing here is a supermarket only between incoming material and the first production process. This is the key interface between the lean manufacturing environment and supply chain management.

SCM ACTION 1

In support of the marketplace material storage concept, procurement must be prepared to ready its suppliers for the change. In most marketplace settings, the inventory locations are designed for package-size storage versus pallet storage. In addition, to provide simplified material handling systems, the handling racks are normally limited to standard sizes. With these requirements SCM has to prepare its suppliers for packaging planning and lot-size compliance.

By establishing and verifying the use of standard package-size and lot-size compliance, procurement can support manufacturing in smoothly introducing marketplace inventory management

1. Rother and Shook, *Learning to See*, p. 44.

with minimal storage rack redesign. Lot-size compliance also aids in min/max inventory level management.

LEAN ACTION 2

Either concurrent with the development of marketplace storage, or immediately following it is the development of incoming inventory quantity control. In a lean manufacturing environment this is accomplished through identifying minimum and maximum inventory levels for each incoming material. This min/max inventory control system is key to the visual nature of lean manufacturing. This concept ensures that deviations from the planned process are easily visually identified in that they fall outside of the norm structure.

The basis for the minimum and maximum levels is derived from the customer demand. A main lean manufacturing tenet is the concept of level production. In this level production system, inventory below the minimum level jeopardizes the plant's ability to manufacture product uninterrupted. Inventory levels above the maximum represent waste in the system. In this case cash is being outlaid to procure and store material that is not needed in the planned manufacturing schedule. While the fundamental process of establishing min/max inventory levels applies to the entire material flow process throughout a lean manufacturing setup, it is at material incoming (or line-side if selected) in which coordinated efforts need to occur with procurement.

SCM ACTION 2

With the establishment of min/max inventory levels, the frequency of inbound material shipments begins to change. The replenishment of min/max levels seldom corresponds to a single weekly or monthly shipment. With increased shipping frequencies there are a number of cost factors that may increase on the supply side. To adequately evaluate these elements,

SCM must conduct formal shipping frequency planning and cost evaluations.

Component suppliers often base their unit price on the planned weekly volumes, with cost based on production run sizes and limited inventory holding. Increasing the shipping frequency may result in suppliers attempting to increase unit price. With adequate evaluation and alternative planning, such cost changes can be eliminated.

Also, increased shipping frequencies can drive up the cost of inbound transportation. Active planning and consolidation of the now smaller and more frequent shipments can eliminate the added costs. Milk-run consolidation, cross-dock activities, or other consolidation efforts can be utilized for these efforts. This issue is much more complicated in the European market, where inbound cost is often born by the supplier.

SUMMARY

This chapter briefly summarized the paired actions necessary do lean work within a company. The paring of lean and supply chain preparation efforts includes the following activities:

- *Lean action 1.* The development of marketplace material storage, which:
    1. Exists between receiving and first manufacturing process.
    2. Doesn't start between processes until continuous flow achievements have been made.
    3. Is the key interface between the lean environment and SCM.
- *SCM action 1* (directly supportive of lean action 1). The preparation of the supply base material delivery systems, including:
    1. Lot size identification and compliance.
    2. Standard packaging development or enforcement.

- *Lean action 2.* The demand-based setting of incoming inventory control levels during which:
  1. Min/max levels are driven from level production, which is the key to the visual nature of lean manufacturing.
  2. Scheduling problems or supplier nonconformance are readily identified.
- *SCM action 2.* The implementation of increased shipment frequencies where:
  1. Smaller lot sizes are driven by closer control of manufacturing space and asset utilization.
  2. The need for formal frequency planning and cost evaluation becomes clear.
  3. Milk-run consolidation, cross-dock, and other logistic issues are addressed.

These primary elements serve as a critical foundation on which production implementation of lean manufacturing systems can begin. Without them, there can only be limited success and a likely retracing of initial efforts as later systems are not supported.

CASE STUDY 16.2

Questions

1. Based on DSW's worldwide lean implantation efforts and progress, and its current financial situation, where should DSW focus its SCM efforts, and in what areas?
2. Based on the implementation focus, what impact might DSW see in commonizing a global approach to lean SCM efforts?
3. How would the SCM organization get in step with the North American lean manufacturing efforts?

Answers

1. DSW's supply chain organization recognized the need to implement its lean SCM efforts in both NA and rest of the world regions. However, this recognition included an understanding that the business, customer, and economic conditions differed in each area. For its North American deployment, DSW selected the "standard environment" initiatives, but also accelerated the initial preparation steps in support of the existing lean effort. In the rest of the world, DSW's lean SCM deployment followed a crisis model. A critical focus of this deployment effort was on immediate savings and cost reductions.
2. The supply chain organization recognized that there was no driving need to have an identical lean implementation profile in each of its regional areas. The need for commonization was determined to be in the tools, strategy, and philosophy of lean SCM deployment. Making every regional SCM group a learning organization was an important objective. As such each region was encouraged to create a unique lean

supply chain environment, but coordinated with other global efforts.

3. The SCM organization was able to get in step with the North American lean manufacturing efforts by accelerating the first lean supply chain actions. By creating a lean material flow, delivery, and inventory system, delivery performance and quality improvements were addressed. The suppliers were provided the reasoning for the process changes, the tools to support the new actions, and the training to implement the tools in a collaborative manner. Whereas previous process changes had been implemented through edict to the supply base, the lean supply chain efforts were addressed through various formal and informal communication, discussion, and decision-making events. The participative approach helped DSW refine its lean SCM efforts, and to facilitate a broader acceptance by the suppliers.

17

Manufacturing Implementation

The implementation of the lean manufacturing process typically occurs on a single product or product line at a time. It is unusual and not recommended to attempt to lean the lines of an entire production facility simultaneously. The lessons learned during the first attempt provide the basis for the second attempt and simplify the third attempt, until the facility as a whole exhibits lean manufacturing techniques. The next paragraphs briefly outline some of the primary actions taken during the manufacturing rollout. Again, the importance is to understand the process and timing of lean manufacturing and how changes in supply chain management can support these efforts.

LEAN MANUFACTURING

To enable all the downstream lean manufacturing activities, the first action which must occur is to determine the required manufacturing time necessary to meet customer demands. Takt time, as the lean manufacturing literature calls it, is simply the calculation of available labor hours divided by the customer demand. Rother and Shook describe this as the initial activity in the development of the lean value stream.[1] Yasuhiro Monden offers detailed meth-

1. Rother and Shook, *Learning to See*, p. 40

ods of translating available work time, customer demand, and other capacity constraints into takt time calculations in his book.[2] Takt time is such a critical factor because its purpose is to maximize the time utilization of the production labor, or stated differently, to use only the time needed to make a part. It is the first step in identifying and eliminating labor waste.

From the development of takt time, the process of continuous flow manufacturing arises. Simply stated, this methodology removes inventories from between the manufacturing processes and delivers a product to the next value-added operation exactly when it is needed. The level of staffing and the work order to be performed is determined by the development of standardized work. Standardized work is a detailed description that tells employees the order in which parts are manufactured to support takt time calculations. Deviations from standardized work result in variance from the takt time, and inhibit the traceability of product defect causes. Monden's book details the benefits obtained by standardized work, and the resulting smoothed production and reduced inventories.[3]

Of all the lean manufacturing processes, this next one is the most widely known. Commonly called just-in-time, the timely availability of the right material, at the right time, in the right quantities, certainly is a cornerstone in lean manufacturing. Although JIT is commonly used in reference to material delivery from a supplier or to a customer, JIT within an operation is equally important. In a successful lean environment, kanban-based material movements facilitate this on-time material availability. Kanban is most easily described as a visual signal sent to the supplying operation

2. Yasuhiro Monden, *Toyota Production Systems*, 3d Ed. (Hingham MA: Kluwer Academic Publishers, 1998), pp. 304–307.
3. Monden, *Toyota Production Systems*, pp. 63–70. Author's note: While production smoothing is a distinct item in TPS practice, which is not detailed here, the ability to achieve production smoothing is greatly dependent on standardized work.

that goods are needed. The kanban signal should be used as the basis of kicking off continued production or material delivery. This kind of material movement is necessary where continuous flow processing is not feasible or when the supply operation is too distant or unreliable. Kanban systems are used most effectively with the use of supermarket or inventory storage between processes, and can provide tremendous advantages over traditional MRP, especially with outside suppliers.[4]

SCM

The changes seen within operations often mirror those with the suppliers. In the development of the material flow strategy, the first element discussed in the lean environment was the placement of a marketplace for incoming components and materials. In the manufacturing implementation, JIT delivery and material availability via a kanban call system were introduced. Now the two can be beneficially paired. With conformance to the packaging specifications, lot compliance, and production smoothing, a supplier kanban can be introduced to achieve component/material JIT. The entire purpose for this is to eliminate a push system of material delivery, and create a pull system. While MRP can represent a pull-type system, it does not reflect manufacturing usage and need in a real-time environment as supplier kanbans do. Quoting Monden, "Although the kanban system is a very effective means to realize the JIT concept, it should not be applied to suppliers without corresponding changes in the overall production system of the user company.[5]

As the component production gets further removed from the ultimate customer, the ability to ensure good product becomes more difficult. The tier one supplier must listen to the final customer, and clearly know the customer's concerns. In the auto-

---

4. Monden, *Toyota Production Systems*, pp. 71–73.
5. Monden, *Toyota Production Systems*, p. 37.

motive industry, customers have been given the ability to warrant the production's quality and usability. However, at the same time, the supplier hasn't yet demonstrated the repeatability to provide acceptable product. The next step in SCM has to be to certify supplier quality through objective quality performance indicators. The ability to do this eliminates the incoming inspection point and delivers the material directly from dock to stock. The development of the objective quality measures (parts per million reject rate, delivery performance, etc.) should drive a supplier stratification methodology[6] that supports the lean manufacturing environment.

The following two SCM initiatives don't necessarily directly correlate to lean manufacturing items; however, the resulting actions provide improved operational support and profitability. The first of these items is the systematic commodity and supplier review activity. As outlined previously, there are many methods by which to accomplish this. The critical factor is driving continued cost, quality, and delivery improvements. Each of these factors increases the level of operational performance. Paired with these continued improvements, and often as a part of systematic commodity strategies, is the consolidation of component and material suppliers. By planning for a controlled and appropriate number of suppliers within a commodity, limited resources can be focused on communicating performance expectations and assisting in driving supplier performance improvement. Competitive benchmarking assessments are detailed in Chapter 11.

Supplier quality performance is often not considered part of SCM responsibility or at least very little is written or mentioned about it in SCM literature. I hold the steadfast position that supplier quality management is as critical in SCM as is purchasing, logistics, and materials management. Poor performance or the lack of root cause resolution leads to a number of downstream SCM activities

6. Wincel, "A Practitioners View," p. 59.

(i.e., expediting activities, premium freight routing, customer containment activities, etc.). It is for this reason that daily supplier quality resolution must be considered a critical element in the joint implementation of SCM and lean manufacturing. In an SCM organization, a supplier quality or development activity serves to assist the operational quality organization in providing for permanent corrective action when additional assistance is needed. While an SQA or SDE activity is not intended to work all the operational supplier issues, their role is to "deep dive" systemic supplier quality problems to protect the operations from a reoccurrence of specific problems. These activities support the implementation of lean manufacturing in that they allow the manufacturing operation to focus its efforts on improving its own activities.

SUMMARY

Figure 17.1 shows a side-by-side pairing for the manufacturing implementation of early lean and SCM steps. Similar comparisons can be established for the materials flow strategy and the ongoing improvements. Through these pairings, the implementation of the true initial efforts of internal lean manufacturing launches can successfully occur.

Manufacturing Implementation

Lean manufacturing actions	SCM Implementation actions
• Takt time calculation	• JIT delivery via kanban system
• Development of standardized work instruction for all operations	• "Dock to stock" part certification (the elimination of incoming inspection)
• Implementation of "pull systems" between processes utilizing kanban	• Systematic commodity and supplier review activity
	• Supplier development focus

Figure 17.1 Manufacturing Pairings

18

Ongoing Improvements

With the careful introduction of the elements described in Chapter 17, lean manufacturing is now in place. Although the steps provide the operational basis for lean, continued refinement will be necessary for life. Supply chain management efforts support the lean rollout, and on their own accord are providing additional benefits to the organization. Now the focus moves to improving the fine points. These elements include working on improving performance measures, trying new equipment, reinforcing the basics, learning new techniques, and learning how to futher create a competitive advantage over the competition in the markets served.

LEAN MANUFACTURING

There is no one in American manufacturing who hasn't heard of kaizen. In Monden's book, he describes kaizen as the method to reduce organizational slack through the "continuous implementation of smaller improvement activities."[1] The organizational slack is the excess amounts of defective product, unused labor time, idle inventories, and other forms of waste or *muda*. The

1. Monden, *Toyota Production Systems*, p. 199.

kaizen activities employed in a lean manufacturing environment are the way to achieve continuous improvement in product setup, product quality, workplace organization and cleanliness, customer satisfaction through delivery performance, and safer working conditions. Improvement in each of these areas provides the opportunity for added profit and business growth.

Many of the main lean manufacturing principles center on the foundation of level production. The ability to achieve this is based on many things, including comprehensive knowledge of customer demand, robust and proactive demand planning systems, and material availability. With the implementation of marketplace pull systems and the use of kanban, it is important to validate the accuracy of material demand signals. Kanban cards become the link between meeting the customer demands and the material available for production. As these systems grow there arises the need to manage the kanban card count. Manufacturing must address this issue to ensure that the cards in the pull system reflect the current demand and level scheduling plan. Loss of cards or overabundance of cards can create a shortage or oversupply of material. Kanban card readers are an effective tool for validating the appropriate number of cards in the system.

In examining the lean manufacturing and SCM co-dependency, it's appropriate to look at the joint manufacturing and supply issue of marketplace and in-process inventory reduction as an ongoing manufacturing improvement. With the lean manufacturing environment, inventories are among the most visible areas of potential waste and improvement. The image of lowering the water in the stream to reveal the stones of opportunity for improvement is a common one applied to inventory reduction. Improvements in manufacturing efficiencies as a result of the lean techniques provide the opportunity to reduce the safety stock on hand.

Figure 18.1 graphically represents the lean manufacturing building blocks utilized by automotive supplier Donnelly Corporation[2] in the "Donnelly Production System." The building represents the base, pillars, and encompassing roof symbolic of the initiatives of a lean manufacturing implementation. Developed by Russ Scaffede, former Senior Vice President of Global Manufacturing Operations at Donnelly, and based on his experience as Vice President of Powertrain Operations at Toyota Motor Manufacturing in Georgetown, Kentucky, the symbols in this graphic drove the various steps of lean implementation at the company.

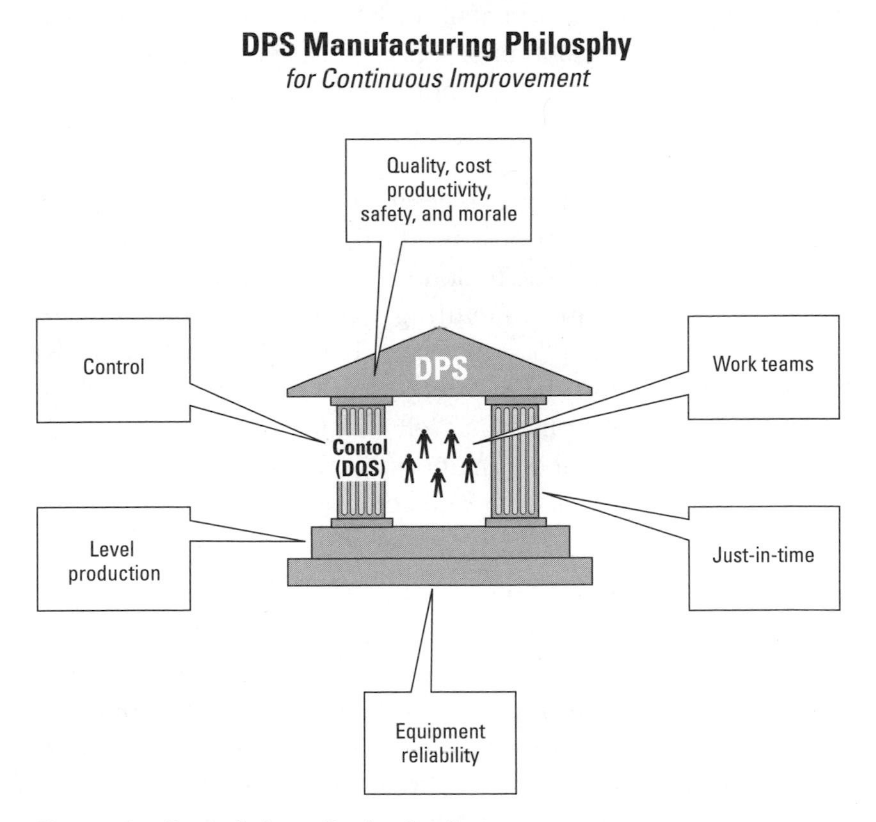

Figure 18.1 Donnelly Lean Production System

2. Donnelly Corporation is now part of Magna International, with the resulting division being called Magna-Donnelly.

SCM IMPROVEMENTS

Purchasing

As the manufacturing operations move beyond the lean manufacturing implementation phase to sustained ongoing improvements, the supply chain management activity is positioned to enter into long-term agreements with its supply base. The definition of a manufacturing strategy and the implementation of SCM strategies define the rules of business in such a clear manner that the risk involved with many multiyear agreements is greatly reduced. These multiyear agreements provide for supplier sourcing continuity, which is a benefit for both the supplier's business planning and the operation's process stabilization efforts, and for ongoing purchase cost/price improvement initiatives; they also demonstrate the sincerity of supply partnerships.

Extending from the multiyear contracts is the ability to select pre-sourced suppliers for new production programs. This ability exists through the clear definition of preferred supply base participants, clarity of manufacturing expectations, quality and price expectations, and jointly planned supplier growth plans. Pre-sourcing simply is the SCM equivalent of capacity planning. By working with suppliers as well as internal customers, efficient use of supplier labor, engineering, financial, and manufacturing resources can be achieved for the benefit of all parties.

Logistics and Distribution

Just as the optimal lean manufacturing layout includes a single customer demand pacing location, SCM becomes truly integrated into a lean manufacturing environment when its distribution activity becomes the pacemaker process. The process of verifying the customer demand and adjusting associated min/max inventory locations can provide the opportunity for the distribution location to become the pull for the rest of manufacturing. By this action, the production demand process is as close to the customer as it can get. Waste is squeezed out of the system throughout the entire value chain, and the process stands or falls based upon its abilities. Material arrives at the distribution point closer to the needing staging window to meet the customer demand, sending back the kanban signal as the material ships.

With the use of the distribution site as the pull signal location, the buildup or shortfall of inventory is isolated in a single visual point throughout the factory, fullfilling the single-piece flow aspects of lean manufacturing. In this situation, the ability to recognize needed changes in inventory level, especially reductions, more quickly occurs. The savings associated with these inventory adjustments can be readily achieved.

Supplier Quality

Again, recognizing that supplier quality is often not thought of as a part of supply chain management, there are ongoing improvement activities that can occur in this area that will affect both traditional SCM activities and manufacturing operations. The first of these is the refinement and implementation of specific supplier performance improvement and measurement metrics. The ability to objectively measure past and current supplier performance in support of the lean and SCM efforts and to proactively address potential shortfalls drives continued improvement in each area.

One of these improved SCM activities is the use of metrics to stratify the commodity supply bases, and to use the stratification in new product source selection. Such stratification provides a direct reward to those suppliers who perform to the highest levels. In addition, the stratification highlights those suppliers who can potentially cause system performance problems, thus enabling proactive corrective measures to be taken.

Product and Program Design

Much of the SCM discussions here are based upon the introduction of a supplier product into series production. However, ongoing SCM improvement must also include the upstream opportunities. The product engineering element cannot be ignored. Through prelaunch value engineering activities, both SCM and manufacturing operations benefit from improved quality levels and product performance. By establishing and meeting component and material performance targets, the need to maintain safety stock and process is minimized. To accomplish these, the SCM activities must employ supplier management evaluation and preparation skills to position the suppliers to fully participate in the activities. Similar value analysis initiatives must also occur and are analogous to the kaizen activities in the production environment.

SUMMARY

When implementing lean processes, many manufacturing organizations begin with the steps described in this chapter instead of ending with them. The desire to eliminate waste throughout the organization, and by connection improve cost, is the driving factor behind this. The danger is that the fundamental skills necessary to support these improvement efforts are not in place. The reductions in organizational slack as evidenced by the elimination of muda (waste), the implementation of kaizen efforts, and manufacturing process refinement are all the elements driving lean improvement.

Some of the additional manufacturing continuous improvement areas include the refinement of material demand signals; reductions to inventory; and better planning mechanisms and technologies, such as automated card readers. These elements continue to match up with changes in SCM such as multiple process improvements in procurement, supplier development, logistics and distribution systems, and product design. The total value chain (or value stream) is expanded beyond the internal environment in these lean refinement actions.

In addition to those mentioned here there are many other lean initiatives and SCM activities that organizations can take advantage of. The key is in understanding the entire value chain or material flow system and how to complement the two disciplines with the focus on improving the value chain for bottom line results.

SUMMARIZING LEAN IMPLEMENTATION AT DSW

As DSW refined the efforts underway within its supply and manufacturing operations, the company began to be recognized as a leader in both lean manufacturing and supply chain initiatives. Frequently, customer organizations would use DSW as a model not only for their other suppliers, but also for their internal operations as well. Training for customer employees would often occur at the DSW facilities, demonstrating the successful implementation of lean initiatives.

Throughout the DSW organization SCM and manufacturing personnel were frequently asked to speak at industry and professional conferences to detail the approaches they used. A number of DSW managers and executives now lead their own businesses in assisting others to implement lean efforts. Even with this attrition, DSW has been able to retain its focus in lean initiatives as both the SCM and manufacturing actions are based on robust processes and not on single individuals.

The lean implementation efforts enabled the company to achieve significant and sustained improvement throughout its divisions, and throughout its worldwide operations. Within supply chain management, DSW has been able to improve net purchase price through the use of its lean supply chain tools. The average reduction has increased each year for the past seven years, and normally exceeds the industry average by 2 to 3 percent per year. The net reductions have now reached 7+ percent per year, without forcing suppliers to take the reduction from their own operating margins. In many cases, as the cost structures have improved and allowed for lower prices, the suppliers' profit margins have increased.

Likewise, supplier quality has improved by over 80 percent during the same period. Coupling the supplier quality improvements with similar internal quality improvements, DSW now achieves "world-class" quality levels—actually moving toward Six-Sigma levels. The inclusion of supplier quality and development as a strategic lean supply chain effort has enabled the creation of a "self-sufficient" supply base, capable of servicing DSW lean requirements.

Finally, DSW's other SCM areas such as logistics, distribution, etc., have recognized their place in overall company efficiency and performance, and have been able to deliver specific EPS (earnings per share) contribution. All SCM efforts now work to treat the supply chain organization as a potential profit center versus a traditional cost center.

DSW continues to refine its lean supply chain efforts. While not every attempt is successful, even the failures provide a learning tool for continued improvement. Like every company initiative, daily events occasionally take focus away from the lean SCM efforts; however, the underlying philosophy of every action continues to be a strategic view of supply chain management.

Index